INSTAHET

Created by the NEEDLECRAFT INSTITUTE

CROCHET IT TODAY – WEAR IT TOMORROW

Graphic Enterprises Inc.

INSTANT CROCHET
TABLE OF CONTENTS

**INSTRUCTIONS FOR HAT ON COVER
SEE PAGE 69**

**INSTRUCTIONS FOR SCARF ON COVER
SEE PAGE 71**

INSTANT CROCHET

Crochet It Today, Wear It Tomorrow!

Crochet is the name of today's fashion game, and everybody can play and win! Crochet is the clever, young, IN thing to do. It's fun and easy to make all the fabulous, new fashions, gifts and accessories everybody loves and wants for practically pennies and in almost no time. Step-by-step pictures and quick, concise directions teach you how to crochet INSTANTLY and professionally...everything from a chignon cap to a poncho to a versatile vest!

We begin with the basics...what you need to know and buy, and how to comprehend crochet language. Chapters 3, 4, and 5 provide picture guides for instant understanding of basic and fancy stitches for right and left-handed crocheters. Next, you'll find loads of helpful hints, tips on finishing finesse, current crochet, how to care for your crochets...and finally, many high-fashion creations to make!

Start now to have the creative time of your life...the young, today way to crochet!

CHAPTER 1
TODAY'S YARNS, HOOKS, ACCESSORIES

THE THREAD OF THE STORY. Yarns and threads are dyed in quantities called "lots" that are numbered. Different lots of the same color often vary in shading. That's why it's important to buy more rather than exactly the amount needed of one dye lot. Stores will take back excess yarn. Be sure to save the paper label from your yarn — it will have both color and dye lot numbers printed on it.

YARN CHART

Natural fiber	cotton, silk, wool
Synthetic	man-made yarns—rayon, orlon plus many other trade names
Blends	natural and synthetic mixtures
Novelties	metallic threads, ribbons, organdy, straw yarn.

If you're a beginner, of course you'll want to use the yarn and needle recommended in your pattern. When you're more experienced, you'll enjoy the creative thrill of inventing your own textures by combining different types of yarns and threads.

CROCHET HOOK SIZES

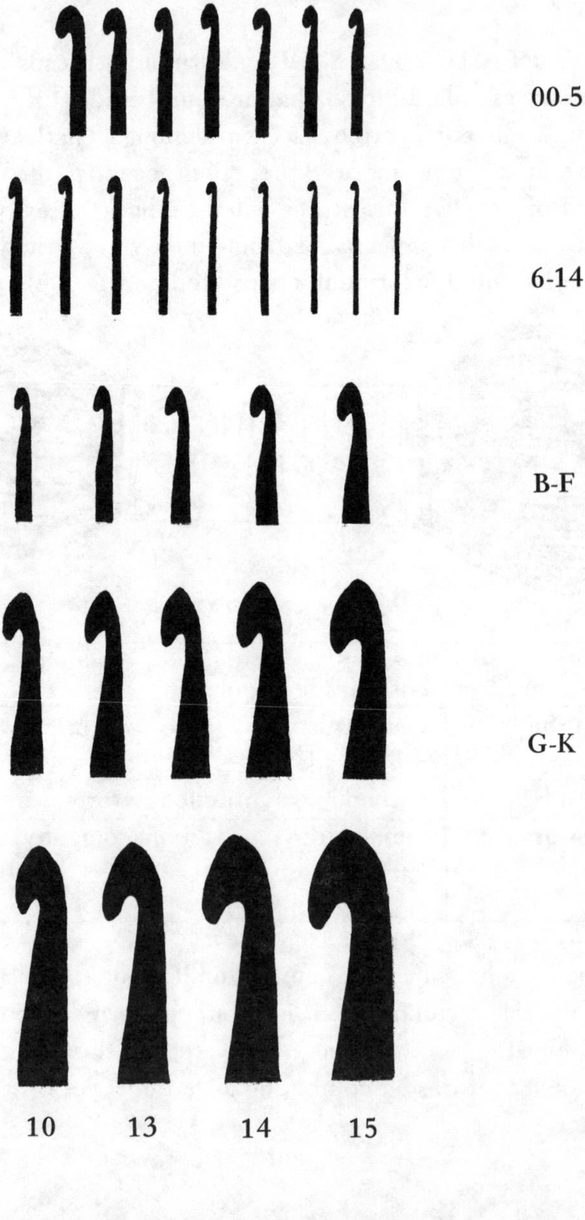

00-5

6-14

B-F

G-K

10 13 14 15

CROCHET HOOKS are made of steel, plastic or aluminum and come in many sizes from fine to large to enable you to work your yarn comfortably and easily. Years ago, afghan hooks were made mainly of wood in contrast to today's plastic or aluminum which is much easier to work with. Aluminum crochet looms which are used for hairpin lace come in sizes from ½" thru 3" or are adjustable from ½" thru 4".

CROCHET HOOK CHART

HOOKS	LENGTH	SIZE	USE	PURPOSE
Steel	5"	American or English 00 thru 14	Fine crochet cotton to heavier cotton or yarn	Tight work
Plastic	5½"	B thru G or 1 thru 6	Synthetic or wool yarns	Flexible work
Aluminum	6"	B thru K or 1 thru 10½	Mercerized crochet and knitting cotton. Cotton rug yarn	Tight work
Plastic or	9"-14"	B thru G 1 thru 10	Synthetic or wool yarns	Mainly used for afghan stitch

TIPS ON TOOLS. Measuring — a rigid 12" ruler plus a cloth or plastic tape measure for curved edges.

Stitch Measure — handy guide for checking your stitch gauge.

Tapestry (crewel or yarn) needle — for seaming and finishing edges. Available now with a ball tip which prevents splitting of the yarn. Use also for any embroidery trim.

Direction Reading Aid — a magnetic bar that magnifies one line of your directions at a time. It's also a ruler for measuring, place marker and buttonhole aid.

DIRECTION READING AID

Yarn End Weaver — a device that provides a quick, easy way to conceal yarn ends and help secure the last stitch.

Other accessories to keep in your crochet kit are a small pair of scissors and safety pins to use as temporary stitch holders. Nylon mesh sweater dryer — use when drying crocheted garments.

YARN END WEAVE

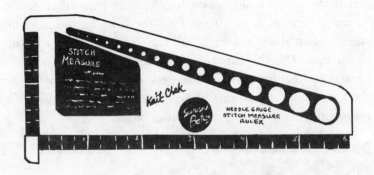

STITCH MEASURE AND NEEDLE GAUGE

CHAPTER 2
MEANINGFUL TERMS AND MEASURMENTS

FOLLOW THE RULES OF THE GAME! — <u>One</u>: Learn the crochet abbreviations below. They tell you what you need to know quickly, and always mean the same in all patterns.

CROCHET SHORTHAND

Ch — chain stitch	dec — decrease
sl st — slip stitch	rnd — round
sc — single crochet	beg — beginning
dc — double crochet	sk — skip
hdc — half double crochet	yo — yarn over hook
tr — treble or triple crochet	pi — picot
long st — long stitch	tog — together
st — stitch	bl — block
sts — stitches	sp — space
lp — loop	pat — pattern
inc — increase	rep — repeat

* Asterisk, ** double asterisk and ◆ diamond indicate that the directions immediately following are to be repeated the number of times given in addition to the first time. Repeat from * 3 times means a total of four. ( ) means — repeat everything within ( ) the amount of times stated directly following the ( ).

(ch 10, skip 6 sts, sc in next st) 4 times means do what is inside ( ) 4 times altogether.

"Work even" means to work in pattern stitch without increasing or decreasing.

<u>Two</u>: Read directions one step at a time as you go, and avoid reading ahead to prevent confusion. It's a good idea to hold your place with a ruler or square of cardboard or "Direction Reading Aid" under the line you are working.

Three: Try to finish the row before you put your crochet down.

Four: CHECK YOUR GAUGE – VERY, VERY, VERY IMPORTANT! If your gauge is not the same as your pattern, your finished article will not be the size you want. BEFORE YOU START, work a chain about 4" long and work in the pattern stitch given with thread or yarn and size hook recommended until your swatch is about 4" deep. Pin along edges to smooth out, and press following blocking directions given in Chapter 8. Count the number of stitches per inch across and the number of rows per inch down. If your sample is larger than 4 x 4", try a size smaller needle until the gauge is reached. If your sample is smaller than 4 x 4", try a size larger needle. Any yarn which works into the gauge may be substituted. Remember, however, that the amount of yarn you need may vary slightly depending on the yarn you choose.

Five: BLOCKING: Stretch and pin each article or section of garments to correct size and shape (following Blocking Charts or measurements given) on a padded surface; cover with a damp cloth and steam (do not press) with a warm iron.

"HOW TO FIND YOUR CORRECT SIZE INSTANTLY"

FIT IS FASHION. "If the dress fits, wear it." If not, why not? It's vital – but not difficult – to choose the right size pattern and make any necessary alterations to fit your figure. Remember, crocheted clothes shape to and follow the contours of the body unlike most fabrics which must be seamed and darted precisely to fit.

Take the measurements recommended here following the "how to" of measuring BEFORE you choose your pattern. Record them on your personal measurement chart so that you can refer to them instantly whenever a question of size arises. In deciding on size, remember that clothes do not fit like the upholstery on a sofa. The body moves, twists, bends. Allowance for ease is given in all patterns to insure comfort. This allowance gives you certain leeway in choosing your pattern size. Although bust size is most often considered the key to determing dress size, it makes no sense to go by your bust measurement if your waist and hips are in a different size category. Again, if your waist is tiny and your hips proportionately much larger, do not go by waist size in choosing skirt and pants patterns. Choose the pattern with the hip measurements corresponding to yours, and make adjustments in the waist.

HOW TO TAKE MEASUREMENTS: Bust (Misses', Juniors, Women) — Around the fullest part of bust.

Shoulder — Back: Measure across back halfway between shoulders and underarms.

Shoulder: Measure across shoulder from arm joint to natural neckline.

Back of Neck: Measure across back of neck from shoulder to shoulder.

Chest (Men and Children): Around fullest part of chest with chest expanded.

Neck to Waist in Back: From bone at back of neck to center of waistline.

Armhole: From top of shoulder in back straight down to one inch below armpit. Measure straight — do not curve in.

Underarm to Waist: From underarm, about one inch below armpit straight down inside arm to wrist bone.

Upper Sleeve Width: Measure around widest part of arm.

Underarm Sleeve Length: Measure from about one inch from armpit straight down inside arm to wrist bone.

Hip: Measure very fullest part of seat. Measure down from waistline to this point at side.

YOUR PERSONAL MEASUREMENT CHART

Your Measurements	Pattern Measurements Closest to Yours	The Difference
Sleeve length . . . ." ... ." . . . ."		
Neck to Waistline . . . ." . . . ." . . . ."		
Bust . . . . ," . . . ." . . . ."		
Shoulder-back . . . ." . . . ." . . . ."		
Waist . . . ." . . . ." . . . ."		
Hip . . . ." . . . ." . . . ."		
Wrist . . . ." . . . ." . . . ."		
Skirt length . . . ." . . . ." . . . ."		
Waist . . . ." . . . ." . . . ."		
Hip . . . ." . . . ." . . . ."		
Pant length . . . ." . . . ." . . . ."		
Measure for bottom width . . . . ." . . . ." . . . ."		

SIZE AND MEASUREMENT CHART

MISSES'	SIZE	6	8	10	12	14	16	18
Bust		$30\frac{1}{2}$	$31\frac{1}{2}$	$32\frac{1}{2}$	34	36	38	40
Waist		22	23	24	$25\frac{1}{2}$	27	29	31
Hip		$32\frac{1}{2}$	$33\frac{1}{2}$	$34\frac{1}{2}$	36	38	40	42
Neck to Waist		$15\frac{1}{2}$	$15\frac{3}{4}$	16	$16\frac{1}{4}$	$16\frac{1}{2}$	$16\frac{3}{4}$	17

WOMEN'S	SIZE	38	40	42	44	46	48	50
Bust		42	44	46	48	50	52	54
Waist		34	36	38	$40\frac{1}{2}$	43	$45\frac{1}{2}$	48
Hip		44	46	48	50	52	54	56
Neck to Waist		$17\frac{1}{4}$	$17\frac{3}{8}$	$17\frac{1}{2}$	$17\frac{5}{8}$	$17\frac{3}{4}$	$17\frac{7}{8}$	18

JUNIOR/TEEN	SIZE	5/6	7/8	9/10	11/12	13/14
Bust		28	29	$30\frac{1}{2}$	32	$33\frac{1}{2}$
Waist		22	23	24	25	26
Hip		31	32	$33\frac{1}{2}$	35	$36\frac{1}{2}$
Neck to Waist		$13\frac{1}{2}$	14	$14\frac{1}{2}$	15	$15\frac{3}{8}$

GIRL'S	SIZE	6	8	10	12	14
Bust		25	27	$28\frac{1}{2}$	30	32
Waist		$22\frac{1}{2}$	$23\frac{1}{2}$	$24\frac{1}{2}$	$25\frac{1}{2}$	$26\frac{1}{2}$
Hip		26	28	30	32	34
Neck to Waist		$11\frac{1}{4}$	12	$12\frac{3}{4}$	$12\frac{1}{2}$	$14\frac{1}{4}$

CHILDREN'S	SIZE	2	4	6	8	10
Chest		21	23	25	27	$28\frac{1}{2}$
Waist		20	21	22	$23\frac{1}{2}$	$24\frac{1}{2}$
Hip		22	24	26	28	30
Neck to Waist		$8\frac{1}{2}$	$9\frac{1}{2}$	11	$11\frac{1}{2}$	$12\frac{1}{4}$

For Half Sizes, use the equivalent Woman's measurements altering length from neck to waistline.
$(32\text{-}34 = 12\frac{1}{2})$; $(36\text{-}38 = 14\frac{1}{2} - 16\frac{1}{2})$; $(40\text{-}42 = 18\frac{1}{2} - 20\frac{1}{2})$; $(44\text{-}46 = 22\frac{1}{2} - 24\frac{1}{2})$.

TO ALTER A PATTERN SIZE: It's simple arithmetic – increasing or decreasing patterns, adding or subtracting rows – to alter a pattern. In overall pattern stitches, calculate alterations by using the stitch gauge equation.

To adjust the length of a vest or jacket, add or subtract the number of rows necessary before armhole is reached.

To adjust the width of a vest or jacket, add or subtract the number of stitches per inch required to adjust each back and front section.

To adjust the sleeve length, add or subtract the number of rows before cap of sleeve is reached.

To shorten or lengthen a skirt, make alteration before hip shaping.

BEFORE YOU START...

Did you crochet your 4x4" gauge?

Did you keep your beginning chain loose enough – unless of course you are told otherwise?

Have you enough yarn to finish?

CHAPTER 3
INSTANT STEP-BY-STEP BASIC STITCHES —
RIGHT HANDED CROCHETER

KNOT-SLIP LOOP

Hold crochet hook in right hand between thumb and index finger; wind yarn around index finger of left hand, leaving about 5" free for forming loop.

Insert crochet hook thru loop from front to back and bring yarn around hook from back to front.

Pull yarn thru loop; pulling cut end tight to form a knot. Knotted loop is called a slip loop which is the beginning of chain stitches.

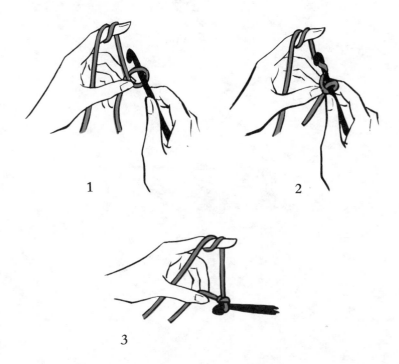

CHAIN STITCH

*Put yarn over hook from back to front and pull thru loop on hook for first chain stitch; repeat from * for desired number of stitches.

1

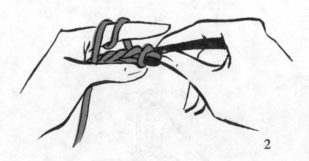

2

SLIP STITCH

Insert hook under one strand only from front to back in 2nd stitch of foundation chain (2 loops on hook), yarn over hook from back to front. Pull yarn thru both stitch and loop at the same time to complete slip stitch.

Work a slip stitch in each stitch along foundation chain.

If slip stitches are not worked in foundation chain, insert hook under 2 top strands of stitch below.

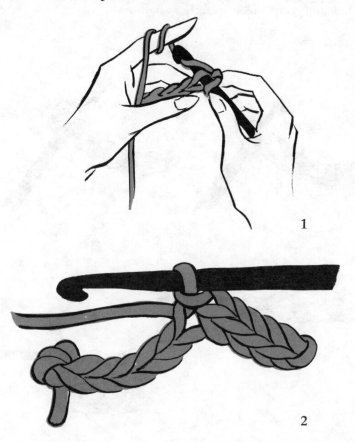

1

2

SINGLE CROCHET

1st Row: Make foundation chain; insert hook in 2nd stitch from hook. Yarn over hook from back to front, pull up a loop thru stitch on hook (2 loops on hook). Yarn over hook again and draw thru 2 loops on hook completing first single crochet. Do second stitch in same manner, inserting hook in next stitch.

2nd Row: Ch 1, turn, insert hook under 2 top strands of sc below and complete sc exactly as before.

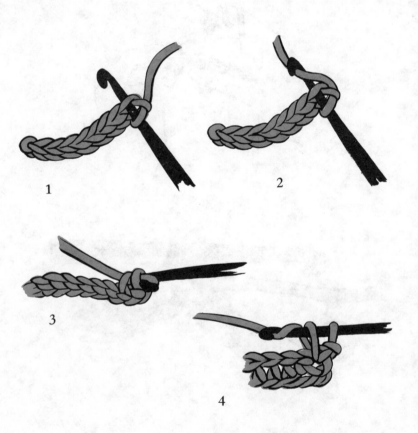

1

2

3

4

HALF DOUBLE CROCHET

1st Row: Make foundation chain; yarn over hook from back to front, insert hook in 3rd st from hook.

Yarn over hook from back to front, pull up a loop thru stitch on hook (3 loops on hook); yarn over hook again and draw thru all 3 loops on hook (completing half dc); work a half dc in each chain st.

2nd Row: Ch 2, turn, (the turning chain usually takes the place of first half dc), skip first half dc, yarn over, insert hook under 2 top strands of half dc below and complete half dc exactly as before. Work a half dc in each half dc of last row, end with a half dc in top st of turning chain of last row.

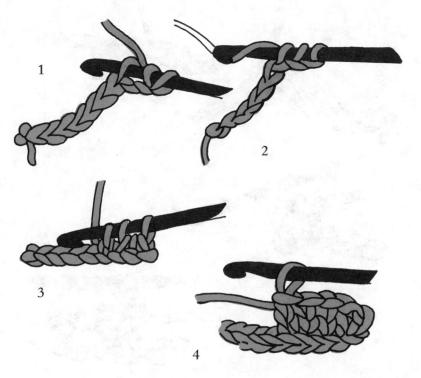

DOUBLE CROCHET

1st Row: Make foundation chain, yarn over hook, insert in 4th stitch from hook (turning chain takes the place of first dc), yarn over from back to front pull up a loop thru stitch (3 loops on hook) yarn over again and draw thru 2 loops only (2 loops still remain on hook). Yarn over hook again and draw thru remaining 2 loops on hook to complete dc. Work a dc in each ch st.

2nd Row: Ch 3, turn, skip first dc of last row, insert hook under 2 top strands in next dc. Work a dc in each dc of row below; end with a dc in top of turning chain.

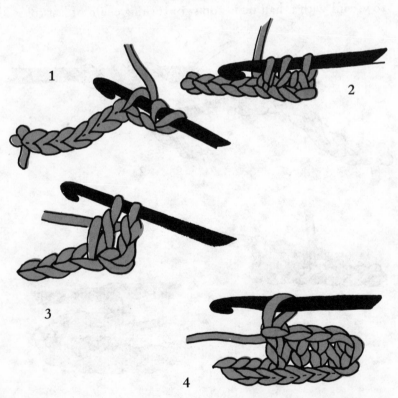

TREBLE CROCHET

1st Row: Make foundation chain, yarn twice around hook, insert hook in 5th stich from hook (turning chain usually takes place of first tr) yarn over hook, pull up a loop thru stitch on hook (4 loops on hook). Yarn over and thru 2 loops. Yarn over and thru 2 loops again. Yarn over and thru remaining 2 loops to complete tr.

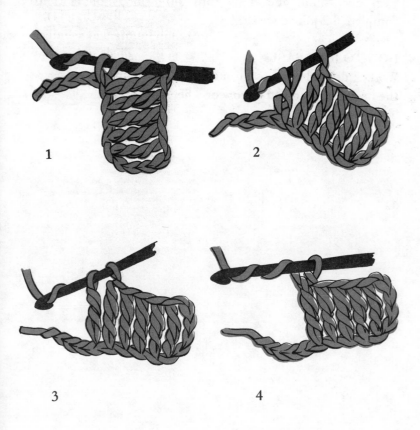

1

2

3

4

HOW TO DECREASE

There are 3 different ways of decreasing stitches.

1. Work every st but end st of row (this will decrease one stitch at end of each row).

2. Skip 1 stitch wherever you want to decrease a stitch.

3. Work joined stitches for decreases as follows: Work first desired stitch up to last step (2 loops on hook), then work 2nd stitch up to last step (you now have 3 loops on hook), yarn over hook and draw thru all 3 loops on hook to complete a 2-joined stitch.

HOW TO INCREASE

Work 2 desired stitches in one stitch of row below; either at the beginning and end of row or wherever desired.

CHAPTER 4
INSTANT STEP-BY-STEP BASIC STITCHES
FOR THE LEFT-HANDED CROCHETER

KNOT-SLIP LOOP

Hold crochet hook in left hand between thumb and index finger; wind yarn around index finger of right hand, leaving about 5" free for forming loop.

Insert crochet hook thru loop from front to back and bring yarn around hook from back to front.

Pull yarn thru loop; pulling cut end tight to form a knot. Knotted loop is called a slip loop which is the beginning of chain stitches.

CHAIN STITCH

*Put yarn over hook from back to front and pull thru loop on hook for first chain stitch; repeat from * for desired number of stitches.

SLIP STITCH

Insert hook under one strand only from front to back in 2nd stitch of foundation chain (2 loops on hook), yarn over hook from back to front. Pull yarn thru both stitch and loop at the same time to complete slip stitch.

Work a slip stitch in each stitch along foundation chain.

If slip stitches are not worked in foundation chain, insert hook under 2 top strands of stitch below.

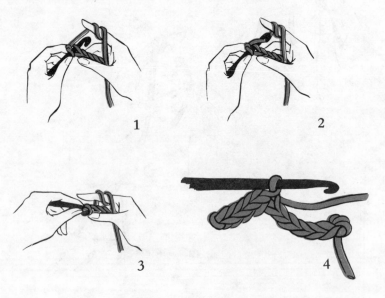

1

2

3

4

SINGLE CROCHET

1st Row: Make foundation chain; insert hook in 2nd stitch from hook.

Yarn over hook from back to front, pull up a loop thru stitch on hook (2 loops on hook).

Yarn over hook again and draw thru 2 loops on hook completing first single crochet. Do second stitch in same manner, inserting hook in next stitch.

2nd Row: Ch 1, turn, insert hook under 2 top strands of sc below and complete sc exactly as before.

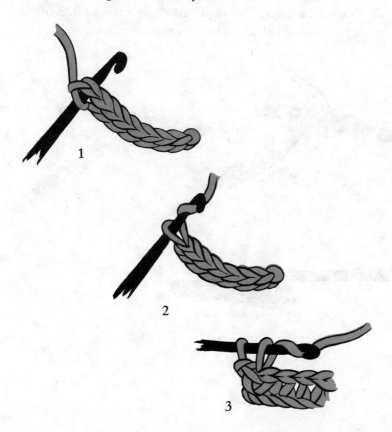

HALF DOUBLE CROCHET

__1st Row:__ Make Foundation chain; yarn over hook from back to front, insert hook in 3rd st from hook.

Yarn over hook from back to front, pull up a loop thru stitch on hook (3 loops on hook); yarn over hook again and draw thru all 3 loops on hook (completing half dc); work a half dc in each chain st.

__2nd Row:__ Ch 2, turn, (the turning chain usually takes the place of first half dc), skip first half dc, yarn over, insert hook under 2 top strands of half dc below and complete half dc exactly as before. Work a half dc in each half dc of last row, end with a half dc in top st of turning chain of last row.

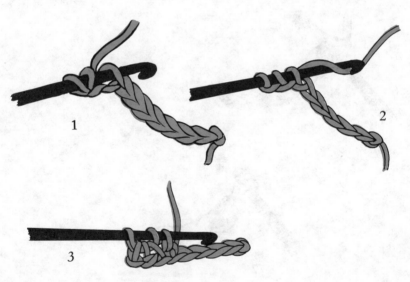

DOUBLE CROCHET

1st Row: Make foundation chain, yarn over hook, insert in 4th stitch from hook (turning chain takes the place of first dc), yarn over from back to front pull up a loop thru stitch (3 loops on hook) yarn over again and draw thru 2 loops only (2 loops still remain on hook). Yarn over hook again and draw thru remaining 2 loops on hook to complete dc. Work a dc in each ch st.

2nd Row: Ch 3, turn, skip first dc of last row, insert hook under 2 top strands in next dc. Work a dc in each dc of row below; end with a dc in top of turning chain.

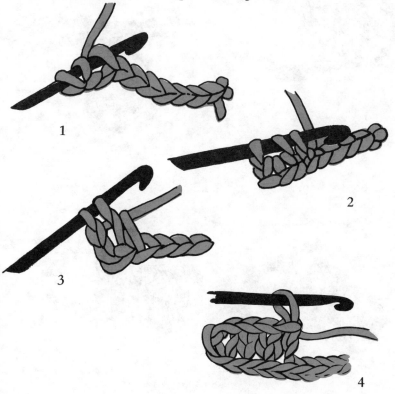

1

2

3

4

TREBLE CROCHET

<u>1st Row:</u> Make foundation chain, yarn twice around hook, insert hook in 5th stitch from hook (turning chain usually takes place of first tr) yarn over hook, pull up a loop thru stitch on hook (4 loops on hook). Yarn over and thru 2 loops. Yarn over and thru 2 loops again. Yarn over and thru remaining 2 loops to complete tr.

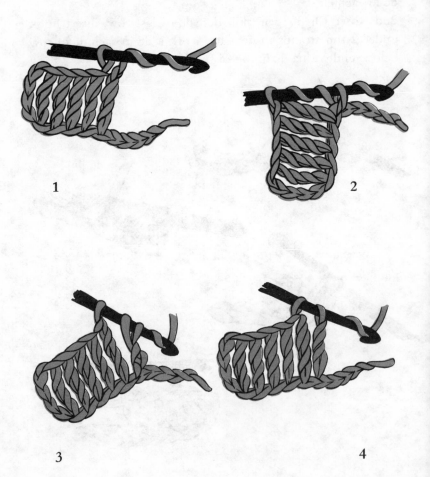

1

2

3

4

CHAPTER 5
INSTANT STEP-BY-STEP FANCY STITCHES

PETAL STITCH — Petal stitches can be made in various sizes and lengths by working more or less joined stitches in one stitch of row below. Illustration shows a 3-joined tr petal. Yarn twice around hook, insert hook in next st, yarn over hook and draw up a loop (4 loops on hook) work (yarn over hook and thru 2 loops) twice * yarn twice around hook, draw up a loop in same st as before (yarn over hook and thru 2 loops) twice; repeat from * once more, yarn over hook and through all 4 loops on hook, ch 1 to complete petal stitch; work as many chain stitches as desired between petal sts.

PUFF STITCH — Make a foundation ch and depending on desired length of puff sts work first st in 4th or 5th st of ch as follows: * yarn over hook draw up a loop in st, pull up loop on hook ½" or longer (YO, draw up another loop same length as before in same st as last loop) as often as required for size of puff, retaining loops on hook, yarn over hook and through all loops on hook, ch 1 to complete puff st, skip 1 st; repeat from * across remaining ch sts.

SLIPPER STITCH – Make a foundation ch, work 1 sc in 2nd st from hook, 1 sc in each remaining chain st. From now on work sc rows back and forth taking stitches over back strand only of each sc of row below.

AFGHAN STITCH – <u>1st Row</u>: Make a foundation ch, draw up a loop in 2nd st from hook, pull loop up so it slides easily over widest part of hook, draw up a loop in each ch st retaining loops on hook. This is half of afghan stitch row, complete row by working loops off as follows: yarn over hook, draw thru one loop * yarn over hook, draw thru 2 loops on hook; repeat from * across. <u>2nd Row</u>: Do not turn, pull out loop on hook which is 1st st of this row, skip 1st vertical bar, insert hook (from right to left) under next vertical bar, yarn over and draw up a loop, draw up a loop in each remaining horizontal bar of last row retaining loops on hook. Complete row same as 1st row.

POPCORN STITCH – Popcorn stitches can be made in various lengths and desired number of stitches. Illustration shows a popcorn st of 5 dc. Work a group of 5 dc in same st, drop loop from hook, insert hook in top of 1st st of group; insert hook in the dropped loop, draw dropped loop thru st on hook, ch 1 tightly to complete popcorn stitch.

RIB DOUBLE CROCHET – <u>1st Row</u>: Make a foundation ch, work 1 dc in 4th st from hook, 1 dc in each remaining ch st. <u>2nd Row</u>: Work 2 dc or as many dc's as desired, then work a rib dc as follows: yarn over hook, insert hook (from right to left) under next st on last row, yarn over hook, draw up a loop under stitch on hook, pull out loops on hook ½", yarn over hook and thru 2 loops, yarn over hook and thru remaining 2 loops (this completes 1 rib dc).

SQUARE MESH – <u>1st Row</u>: Make a foundation chain divisible by 3 plus 8 extra sts, work 1 dc in 8th st from hook; * ch 2, skip 2 ch sts, 1 dc in next st; repeat from * across chain, ending with 1 dc in last ch st. <u>2nd Row</u>: Ch 5, turn, skip first dc and ch 2, 1 dc in next dc of row below; * ch 2, skip ch 2 of row below, 1 dc in next dc; repeat from * across row, end with 1 dc in 3rd st of turning chain; repeat last row thruout.

OPEN BLOCK – <u>1st Row</u>: Make a foundation chain divisible by 12 plus 6 extra sts, work 1 dc in 4th st from hook, 1 dc in each of next 2 ch sts; * ch 2, skip next 2 ch sts, 1 dc in each of next 4 ch sts; repeat from * across remaining chain sts. <u>2nd Row</u>: Ch 5, turn, skip 1st 3 dc; * 1 dc in next dc of row below, 2 dc in next (ch 2) space, 1 dc in next dc, ch 2, skip next 2 dc; repeat from * across row, end with 1 dc in top of turning ch 3. <u>3rd Row</u>: Ch 3, turn; * 2 dc in next (ch 2) space of row below, 1 dc in next dc, ch 2, skip next 2 dc, 1 dc in next dc; repeat from * across row, end with 2 dc in last space, 1 dc in 3rd st of turning ch 5. Repeat last 2 rows thruout.

LOOP STITCH – (can be used for fringe) – Cut a strip of cardboard as wide as you want the loops to be long and about 3" long. Make a foundation chain, work a loop st as follows: hold cardboard in back of chain, insert hook in 2nd st from hook, wind yarn around cardboard from back to front, yarn over hook and thru 2 loops on hook (see Detail 1); work another loop st like this in each remaining chain st (see Details 2 and 3). When cardboard is completely filled with loops, slip all but last 2 loops off cardboard and continue working until all loops are completed (see Detail 4). If joined loops are desired (see Detail 5) do not break off yarn but work chain sts the length of last loop; working along looped end of loops work 1 sc in each loop; break off.

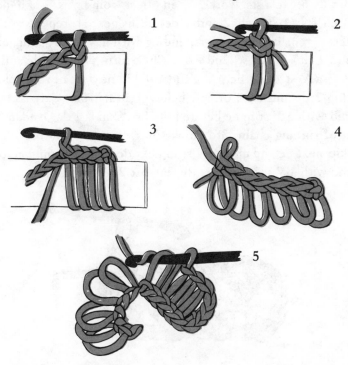

PICOT – Ch 3 or more; work an sc in 1st ch st made (to form picot). Sometimes a picot is worked in top of a st; in that event ch 3 (or more), a sc in top of last st before chain.

V STITCH – 1st Row: Make a foundation chain divisible by 3 plus 6 extra sts, work 1 dc in 6th st from hook; * skip next 2 ch sts (1 dc, ch 2 and 1 dc) all in next st; repeat from * across remaining chain sts, ending with a V st of (1 dc, ch 2 and 1 dc) in last st. 2nd Row: Ch 3, turn, skip first dc and ch 2; * a V st of (1 dc, ch 2 and 1 dc) in next dc of row below, skip 1 dc and ch 2 of row below; repeat from * across row, end with a V st in dc before last V st, skip last dc, 1 dc in 3rd st of turning chain. 3rd Row: Ch 5, turn, 1 dc in first dc; * skip next dc and ch 2, a V st in next dc; repeat from * across, end with a V st in last dc. Repeat last 2 rows thruout.

STAR STITCH – <u>1st Row</u>: Make a foundation chain divisible by 2 plus 5 extra sts, skip 1st ch and draw up a loop in each of next 4 ch sts (always pull up loops ½") yarn over and draw thru all 5 loops on hook, * ch 1 for eye of star stitch, pull loop on hook out 1/2", draw up a loop thru eye of star st, another one thru back of last loop of star st just made and another one in each of next 2 ch sts, yarn over and thru all 5 loops on hook; repeat from * across remaining ch sts, ending with ch 1 for eye which completes last star stitch. <u>2nd Row</u>: Ch 3, turn, skip 1st ch, draw up a loop in each of next 2 ch sts, draw up a loop thru eye of 1st star st of row below and another one thru side loop of same star st; yo and thru all 5 loops on hook, * ch 1, pull up loop on hook, draw up a loop thru ch 1 (eye of star stitch just completed) another one thru back of last loop of same star st, draw up another one thru eye of next star st of row below and one more loop thru side loop of same star st of row below, yo and thru all 5 loops on hook; repeat from * across row. This row forms pattern stitch; repeat last row thruout.

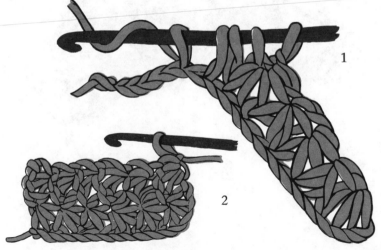

SHELL STITCH — <u>1st Row</u>: Make a foundation ch, divisible by 6 plus 4 extra sts, 1 dc in 4th st from hook, 1 more dc in same st as last dc; * skip next 2 ch sts, 1 sc in next st, skip next 2 ch sts, a group of 5 dc in next st; repeat from * across ch, ending with a group of 3 dc in last chain stitch. <u>2nd Row</u>: Ch 1, turn, 1 sc in 1st st; * skip next 2 dc, a group of 5 dc in next sc, skip next 2 dc, 1 sc in next dc (center dc of group); repeat from * across row, ending with skip 2 dc, 1 sc in top st of ch 3. <u>3rd Row</u>: Ch 3, turn, 2 dc in 1st sc; * 1 sc in center dc of next group of 5 dc, a (5 dc) group in next sc; repeat from * across row, ending with a group of 3 dc in last sc. These last 2 rows form pattern stitch; repeat for desired length.

CHAPTER 6
HELPFUL HINTS

THE WIND-UP. If your yarn does not come in a pull skein, you'll have to wind it into a ball. Don't wind too tightly for you may stretch the natural elasticity of the yarn. Here's how to do it. Wind several strands around four fingers. Slip the yarn off your fingers into a little wad, and continue winding over ball and four fingers, changing directions and guiding the yarn from the skein gently. Your ball of yarn should be soft enough to press in when touched.

JOINING: There are three ways to join the end of a ball of yarn to a new ball. Try to join at the end of a row rather than in the middle.

1. At the end of a row: Leaving about 2" dangling from both ends, knot new and old yarn together. Continue to crochet with new yarn. When you seam pieces together, "work in" loose ends one at a time. Thread one end on a needle, and weave thru crochet. Repeat with other end. Cut off excess.

2. In the middle of a row: Leaving about 2" dangling from both ends, knot new and old yarn together. Continue to crochet with new yarn. Later, thread a needle with one end and weave carefully thru crochet. Do the same with other end weaving in opposite direction.

3. <u>Splicing</u>: Unravel about 2" of new and old threads, and cut strands unevenly. Lay strands of both ends together, and roll trying to copy twist of yarn as much as possible. You'll find this method makes a very strong "join".

RIPPING AND RE-USING RIPPED YARN:

1. Rip seams with embroidery or manicure scissors with curved tips.

2. Beginning with last stitch, rip each piece gently and wind around a book or sturdy cardboard about 12" long.

3. Tie skein in several places. Remove from book or cardboard.

4. Wash yarns of natural fibers in lukewarm water with mild soap suds or in cold water with a cold water soap. Wash synthetic yarns by hand in lukewarm water with soap or detergent. Do not rub. Use fabric softener in final rinse. Hang strands up and weight of water will take out wrinkles. While yarn is still wet, stretch out kinks with your fingers.

5. When dry, roll into balls.

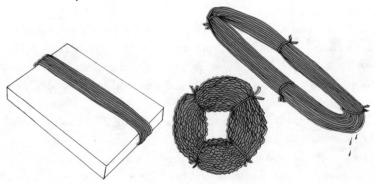

CHAPTER 7
FINISHING FINESSE

BLOCKING MAKES IT BEAUTIFUL — Blocking is the most important step in transforming crocheted pieces into a fashion with professional fit and finesse. Always block pieces separately <u>before</u> seaming together unless your instructions tell you otherwise.

To block, place crocheted piece right side down on a well padded surface or ironing board. Pin with rustproof pins to correct length and width given in pattern. Cover with damp cloth and gently lower iron, slowly allowing steam to penetrate. Do not press, or even touch. This technique is especially recommended for fluffy yarns, popcorn stitches or raised patterns. Never press iron down, keep in one place or slide along piece. When two pieces have the same measurements, pin down one piece and block. Place reverse piece on top (right side up), and block. Allow pieces to dry completely before removing pins.

RESHAPING — Cut a paper pattern to the exact shape of the garment. Launder according to directions in Chapter 10, and pin to paper pattern on a flat, padded surface. For yarns that absorb a great deal of water such as boucle, place garment in lingerie bag or pillow case, and put into spin-dry cycle of washing machine — or roll in terry towel to absorb water. Then, allow garment to completely dry before unpinning.

FINISHING — Pin and baste side and shoulder seams. Try on, and make minor alterations. Put right sides together facing each other, and overcast together on wrong side. Use a tapestry needle with matching yarn. Remember that your seaming should have the same elasticity as your crochet work. Be sure to match pattern stripes, ribs or any decorative rows of stitching carefully at the seam. If garment has a natural waistline, it is advisable to stabilize it by sewing oval elastic to inside waistline of dress.

SEAMING STRATEGY – 1. Overcast together front and back sections starting at underarm and shoulder.
2. Overcast together underarms of sleeves. For smooth-fitting, set in sleeves, first pin center top of sleeve to shoulder seam with right sides facing.
3. Pin underarm seam to underarm seam of garment.
4. Pin upward from underarm seam toward shoulder seam easing in fullness each side of the top of sleeve.

FIVE EASY, ELEGANT WAYS TO EDGE IT – Edgings finish fashions and accessories with a graceful flourish. Use a matching yarn for today's jiffy, jumbo designs. Here are 5 INSTANT EDGINGS.

FOLD-OVER BRAID BINDING – Slip pre-folded binding over edge to be bound. Machine stitch thru all 3 layers.

LEATHER BINDING – If binding is not pre-cut, then cut to twice the width wanted. Fold binding over edge allowing a little more at underside. Machine stitch (8 sts to inch) thru all layers.

 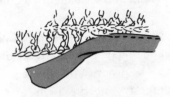

FOLD-OVER BRAID BINDING   LEATHER BINDING

SHELL STITCH EDGING – <u>1st Row</u>: Make a chain desired length, having a number of stitches divisible by 6 and 2 extra sts; 1 sc in 2nd st from hook; * ch 2, skip 2 ch sts, 1 sc in next st; repeat from * along chain. <u>2nd Row</u>: Ch 1, turn, 1 sc in first sc, * skip next (ch 2) space, 5 dc (a shell) in next sc, skip next (ch 2) space, 1 sc in next sc; repeat from * across row; break off.

SHELL STITCH EDGING

SINGLE CROCHET EDGING – Follow directions for single crochet given under Basic Stitches Page 20. Make 2 rows of single crochet and work 3 single crochet in 1 single crochet of row below for a corner where necessary.

SINGLE CROCHET EDGING

PUFF STITCH EDGING – Make a chain desired length, having a number of stitches divisible by 3 and 4 extra stitches; 1 dc in 4th st from hook; * work a puff st in top of last dc as follows: pull out loop on hook ½", yarn over hook, draw up a ½" loop in last dc made (yarn over hook, draw up ½" loop in same dc as last loop) 3 times, yarn over hook and draw thru all 9 loops on hook, ch 1, to complete puff st, 1 sc in same dc as puff st, skip next ch st, 1 dc in each of next 2 ch sts; repeat from * along chain; break off.

PUFF STITCH EDGING

CROCHETED BUTTONS – Use a flat button or wooden button mold.

Material	Hook
No. 30 Cotton	10 Steel Crochet Hook
Mercerized Crochet & Knitting Cotton	8 Steel Crochet Hook
3-ply Fingering Yarn	2 or C Plastic
Sport Yarn or (4-ply Fingering Yarn)	4 or E Plastic

Work button covers in single crochet tightly so that the crochet covers the mold completely. Follow directions for all buttons; they are worked round and round.

1ST ROUND: Ch 3, join with a sl st into a ring; 6 sc into ring;

2ND ROUND: 2 sc in each sc of last round; (12 sc in round).

3RD ROUND: * 1 sc in next sc, 2 sc in next sc (an increase); repeat from * 6 times (18 sc in round).

Depending on the size of the button to be covered, stop here or continue to increase 6 sc in each round in same manner as in 3rd round having 1 more sc in each sc group before increases than in previous round (check 3rd round for increase). When flat crocheted circle is the same size as button, work 2 rounds even. Insert button mold into crocheted piece and decrease as follows: * 1 sc in next sc, skip next sc; repeat from * around and around until button is completely covered; break off, leaving enough yarn for sewing on button.

BUTTONHOLES – 1. Work chain stitches the desired length of buttonhole starting about ½" from edge of garment. Crochet over chain stitches to complete buttonhole usually with single crochet or, if necessary pattern stitch.

2. Use grosgrain ribbon for binding (same or a harmonizing color) on wrong side to reinforce buttonholes. Of course, you have already blocked your garment. To keep the ribbon from shrinking, press it with a steam iron or without steam under damp press cloth.

3. Sew ribbon flat with a back or overhand stitch at edge. Sew inner edge.

4. With point of small scissors, carefully slash ribbon under each buttonhole. Turn under raw edges of ribbon, and stitch in place with small slip stitches.

LOOPS – 1. Make a chain stitch loop. Reinforce with single crochet by working single crochets into chain loop until you have a firm edge.

2. Break off yarn end. Thread yarn on tapestry needle and weave ends securely into wrong side of garment.

ZIPPERS IN A ZIP! – 1. Crochet one row of single crochet around edge of opening for zipper, being careful to keep edge straight.

2. Face with ribbon binding on wrong side to prevent strain on crocheted stitches.

3. Pin closed zipper into place taking care not to stretch edges as you pin.

4. Sew zipper into place by hand with matching cotton thread. Make sure crocheted edge covers zipper tape. If it shows, work an extra row of single crochet after zipper is in.

FRINGES – 1. Wind yarn loosely around a cardboard a little longer than half the length you want the fringe to be. Cut yarn at one end.

2. Fold one or several strands of yarn in half to form a loop.

3. Working along edge of crochet, insert crochet hook from back to front in each stitch of first row using a single strand or spacing if using several strands.

4. Draw loop thru. Draw loose ends thru loop and pull tightly to form a knot.

TASSELS – 1. Cut a square of cardboard a little larger than the size you want your tassel to be.

2. Wind yarn around cardboard until tassel has the plumpness you want.

3. At one end of the cardboard, tie off strands of yarn securely with a double strand leaving 3" ends. Slip tassel off cardboard.

4. About ¼" below top or at point desired, wind a strand of yarn around several times.

5. Cut thru bottom and trim.

6. Thread a tapestry needle with yarn ends, and sew tassel securely in position on article.

CHAPTER 8
LINE IT TO KEEP IT SHAPELY

A lining provides comfort and luxury, and is extremely practical because it keeps a garment in shape, and helps it wear longer. It's very important to line ribbon and lacy crochets. Do not use bulky or stiff fabrics for linings. Batiste, China silk, Sibonne, crepe are all excellent, stabilizing lining materials. When stretch is important, line the garment with tricot so as not to restrict the stretch. Line swim suits with opaque tricot – the stretch going around the body. It is not necessary to line the top unless it is crocheted in a very loose, open stitch. If a lining is required, a purchased bra cut to fit the front works very well. Notions counters make special bra linings and cups available.

There are two types of linings – the loose, slip lining that is attached only at the shoulders or at the waist of a skirt or pants, and the attached lining. You can use your blocked garment to make a paper pattern for a lining, or your Basic Dress Pattern.

Remember that fabric does not have the same "give" as crochets so you'll have to provide for shoulder and bust darts as well as back and elbow ease. Allow a 5/8" seam allowance for your lining.

TO LINE A JACKET – 1. Cut paper pattern from blocked jacket, and cut out one right and one left front. If your jacket has a button closing in front, stop lining short of buttons and buttonholes.

2. Sew bust darts in front.

3. Cut out back. Sew shoulder darts in back.

4. Baste a center back pleat 2" down from neckline to give needed ease across the back.

5. Join front and back sections at sides.

6. Press seams open.

7. Pin and sew lining to inside of jacket. Overlap lining at shoulders. Turn under raw edges of front and slip-stitch together. The lower edge of the lining and jacket should not be attached but should hang freely.

8. Try on jacket for fit and length of lining hem. Turn up and catch-stitch lining hem. Make lining hem about 1/2" shorter than jacket.

TO LINE SLEEVES – 1. Cut sleeves with back seam of sleeve 1" longer than front. Gather excess at back seam for about 3" around elbow area to allow ease of movement.

2. Run a gathering thread along cap of sleeves. Sew underarm seams of sleeves, and press open. With wrong side out, push sleeve lining into jacket sleeve.

3. Turn under raw edges and baste sleeves into armholes easing gathers of sleeve cap into armhole. Slip stitch sleeve lining onto jacket lining catching jacket to prevent shifting.

4. Try on jacket. Turn lining up at lower edge of each sleeve even with crochet edge. Slip stitch 1" up from crocheted edge to prevent pulling.

TO LINE A SKIRT – 1. Cut a paper pattern from blocked garment allowing width of hip at waistline.

2. Cut out lining. Join front and back sections with 5/8" seam at sides leaving top open 8" on both sides. Press seams open. Narrow hem raw edges of seams along openings at top of seams. Remember that the wrong side of the lining should face the wrong side of your crocheted skirt.

3. Turning under 5/8" seam allowance, stretch crocheted skirt top so lining gathers evenly to top of skirt along bottom of casing for elastic. The lining front should be centered on skirt front – lining back centered on skirt back. Lining will

have 8" long openings at either side of skirt. These will allow for extra stretch needed to get skirt over your head without requiring a zipper.

4. Turn under 1/4" along lower edge of skirt lining and stitch. Turn up hem of lining to be 1" shorter than hem of crocheted skirt. Catch-stitch lining hem so that lining hem hangs free of crocheted skirt.

TO LINE A DRESS (SLIP METHOD) — 1. Cut a paper pattern from blocked garment or your Basic Dress Pattern

2. Sew bust and shoulder darts (ease needed since fabric lining doesn't stretch like the crocheted body).

3. Join front and back with 5/8" seams at sides. Press seams open.

4. Slip-stitch shoulders into shoulders of dress.

5. Try on dress, and hem lining 1/2" shorter than dress.

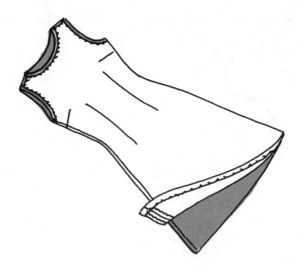

UN-ATTACHED LINING

TO LINE A DRESS (ATTACHED LINING) — Do not join crocheted pieces before making lining.

1. Cut a paper pattern from each blocked piece. Allow sleeve ease and make shoulder back and bodice darts as recommended above.

2. On flat surface, place lining pieces over crocheted pieces with wrong sides facing.

3. Smooth flat and pin in place.

4. Stitch both pieces together all the way around each part as far down as waistline. Allow skirt to hang free.

5. Check to make sure that the lining lays flat on dress without wrinkles.

6. Assemble garment treating both layers as if they were one.

7. Below waistline sew dress and lining seams separately.

8. Try on garment for hemline. Cut away lining at hemline to eliminate excess bulk.

9. Turn up lining and stitch. Lining hem hangs free of crocheted hem.

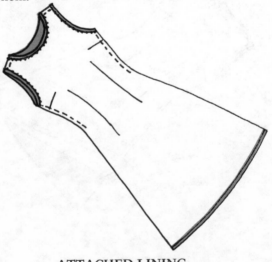

ATTACHED LINING

CHAPTER 9
CROCHETING WITH RIBBON, SEQUINS, BEADS

RIBBON – For pure luxury and beauty, crochet something with ribbon – perhaps a shell with or without sleeves, evening dress or blouse. You can buy silk, rayon or nylon ribbon in textures as crisp as taffeta or organdy, or soft as crepe. Ribbon can be combined with metallic threads and yarns to create unique couture effects.

Handling ribbon is different from other yarns. Your stitch gauge is very, very important.

TO BLOCK SWATCH –

1. Straighten any stitches not lying flat.
2. Press swatch on padded surface using light, damp press cloth and steam iron. Never, never press directly on ribbon. However, the degree of loft will depend on your individual taste. Measure your blocked swatch against the gauge given and if it accords with the stitches per inch given, proceed with your work.

Ribbon is most often crocheted flat although there are some patterns that use ribbon in the same way as yarn. Always work loosely, keeping ribbon flat and pull out several yards of ribbon ahead of your crocheting. If it is necessary to rip, or you find wrinkles or twist marks, run the ribbon over a hot electric light bulb. Instantly your ribbon will be smooth and flat.

JOINING: – To start a new wheel or spool, overlap ends of ribbon you are crocheting about 3/4" onto new ribbon. Turn under raw edges of both, and sew together with small stitches.

FINISHING – Ribbon pieces are seamed together like fabric, with a 3/8" seam allowance. Follow directions in Chapter 2 on fitting and altering. You can seam by hand or machine with matching silk, rayon or nylon thread depending on the fiber of your ribbon. If you sew your seams by hand, use a running backstitch. With sewing machine, use a small zigzag stitch or regular stitching. Finish open edges like hems, sleeves and neck edges with single crochet, and press.

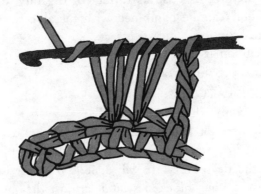

CROCHETING WITH BEADS AND SEQUINS – Beads and sequins are usually crocheted into a garment from the wrong side. It's important to use a yarn that slides easily through the hole. Use fine crochet cotton for seed beads, heavier crochet cotton, 3-ply fingering yarn or metallic yarn for medium size pearls, a heavier yarn for wooden beads.

Sequins come strung on a fine thread, or loose and are flat or cupped in shape. If they're strung on a double strand remove one strand. They are usually crocheted in with a chain loop and single crochet. Keep loose sequins in a shallow dish, and string using a fine needle and doubled sewing thread. If you are working with crochet cotton, you may be able to thread sequins directly onto the cotton and eliminate the stringing step. Pick up sequins with point of needle, and push onto thread making sure inside of cup faces needle.

PAILLETTES – Plastic paillettes come in a wide range of colors and iridescent tones. They can be round, oval or diamond shaped, and have a large hole near one end. Whenever possible, slide the paillette directly onto the yarn without stringing. You can also insert the crochet hook right through the hole and crochet into garment.

THREADING SEQUINS ONTO YARN – Tie end of stringing thread around yarn. Slide sequins onto yarn carefully allowing yarn to fold back as shown. Depending on how many sequins are called for in your pattern, string from one to five strands onto yarn at a time. When last sequins are used, cut yarn about 5" from work and repeat threading sequins onto yarn.

THREADING SEQUINS ONTO YARN

STRINGING BEADS – Thread a needle that is fine enough to slide through bead hole with nylon thread. Knot securely, and string about 15" of beads. Remove needle, and tie end of thread tightly around crochet yarn with a small knot. Slide beads over knot and onto crochet yarn. Slide as many beads onto crochet yarn as you need to work on. Cut off nylon bead thread.

STRINGING BEADS

HAIRPIN LACE – (1) Remove cross bar from bottom of loom. Loom is held with round end up. Make a loose slip loop (half the size of width of loom); drop loop off hook and slip it onto the left prong of loom; tighten knot; replace cross bar.

(2) Wind yarn around right side of loom from front to back and insert hook under front strand of loop on left hand prong. Pick up yarn with crochet hook and bring it through loop, ch 1.

(3) Turn loom from right to left side toward you, winding yarn around right side prong and passing shank of hook through loom at the same time, insert hook under front strand of loop on the left hand prong.

(4) Pick up yarn with crochet hook and pull through loop (2 loops on hook); yarn over hook and through both loops on hook.

Repeat (3) and (4) for desired number of loops.

HAIRPIN LACE

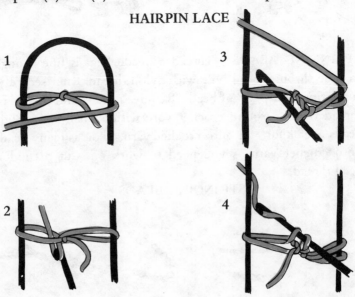

54

CHAPTER 10
CARE OF CROCHETS

LAUNDERING CROCHETS — Find out when you buy your yarn whether it is washable or should be dry-cleaned, and if it is colorfast.

If working in multicolor and doubt their colorfastness, add a little vinegar to the final rinse to help "Set" the color. Or — if your garment has a light collar on a dark dress, place a paper towel between the two layers until dry to prevent bleeding.

WASHING WOOLENS

1. Shake out dust.
2. Use any product labeled especially for fine woolens — cold water soap, mild soap powder, liquid detergent, and lukewarm water.
3. Squeeze suds through article but do not rub. If the article is very soiled, wash and rinse several times rather than using a larger quantity of the washing product just once.
4. Rinse thoroughly, and be sure no suds remain in article.
5. Never hold up a garment that is soaking wet because the weight of the water can stretch it out of shape.
6. Roll in a turkish towel to absorb excess moisture.
7. Follow directions for reshaping in Chapter 8.

WASHING SYNTHETICS

1. Turn article to wrong side. Use warm water and any mild soap or detergent.
2. Wash by hand or machine. If washing by hand, follow steps 3 to 7 above.

WASHING COTTON

1. Make thick suds with hot water and mild soap powder.
2. Add cold water until suds are lukewarm.
3. Place cotton lace garments in suds, squeeze gently until clean.
4. Rinse several times in lukewarm water to remove all soapy residue.
5. Rinse in cold water.
6. Roll in a turkish towel to remove excess moisture.

RE-SHAPING CROCHETS – Re-shape crocheted fashions after laundering this way:

1. Cut a paper pattern to the exact size and shape of the garment.
2. Launder according to directions for fiber (wool, cotton, synthetic) in this chapter.
3. To remove excess moisture, you can roll crochet in terry cloth towel and squeeze gently. OR place crochet in a nylon mesh bag, and put in washing machine on spin-dry cycle.
4. Lay paper pattern on a padded surface or nylon mesh dryer. Shape garment following paper pattern. Leave until completely dry.

CARE OF CROCHETS – Do not hang crocheted fashions on a clothes hanger. This distorts the garment. If hanging is a must, hang over a plumply padded rod or a sturdy wooden hanger. It's preferable to fold and lay crochets in a drawer or on a shelf with tissue paper placed between the folds to avoid creasing.

CHAPTER 11
INSTANT TIPS!

To hold shape at back of neck or on shoulder, stitch narrow seam tape to neck and shoulder seams.

To fit a skirt at the waist using elastic in a casing, work about 1" of single crochet around top, then turn work to wrong side without breaking the thread. Make a chain of 1" and carry it diagonally to the base of the band made of single crochet; work a slip stitch into the base of a single crochet. Make another chain of the same length and carry this chain to the top edge and fasten in same manner. Repeat around band. Run a piece of elastic 3/4" wide thru beading, and sew ends together.

Never, never put a crocheted article in the sun to dry.

To take the place of a stitch-and-row counter when you are working with a number of different pattern stitches, you can use an add-a-matic clicker that records dollars, dimes and cents at the grocery store. It's also great for recording rows as well as other counting within a pattern.

To make sure that both sides of a vest, jacket or coat are the same length when finished, make sure you have the same number of single crochets on each edge. To help you count, try putting in a pin after each 10 stitches. This will help you keep track of the total number of stitches worked.

For a skirt worked in the round with a casing at the waist, avoid sitting out the back by moving skirt around at waist each time you wear it.

If you don't fully line a skirt, line the back to below the seat to help keep the shape.

Make yourself a ribbon wheel by sliding a needle or pencil thru hole in wheel or spool and propping on drawer or tissue box so ribbon rolls off easily.

Baste together a Basic Dress in muslin to fit your personal measurements and use flat as a master pattern to check the fit of a crocheted dress, coat, blouse or jacket, always remembering that your crochet garment will stretch where your fabric garment will not.

ADDITIONAL INSTANT TIPS

To make rolled edges lie flat and support sagging borders, work single crochet along edges being careful to keep edge straight. Work 2 to 3 stitches in corners.

When crochet directions tell you to work a certain number of inches, you need to measure your work accurately. Lay crochet down on a flat surface. Using a ruler, place the end on the crochet piece and measure down to the starting point, or to the point indicated in the directions. Do not stretch your work – just smooth it out gently. Above all, don't be tempted to try to make it measure more than it does – you may make a crucial error that will force you to rip and start over again.

CHAPTER 12

LEARNER'S PONCHO
MATERIALS NEEDED

6 ozs. of 4-ply Knitting Worsted in each of 2 contrasting colors or 2 shades of one color; a No. 6 or G Plastic Crochet Hook.

GAUGE – WORKING IN SINGLE CROCHET
4 sts = 1 inch
4 rows = 1 inch

FIRST SECTION (14" X 30")

1ST ROW: With 1st color, ch 121 (this chain should measure 30-1/4" without stretching), 1 sc in 2nd st from hook (insert hook in next st, yarn over hook, draw up a loop, yarn over hook, draw through 2 loops on hook for an sc), 1 sc in each st across chain (there are 120 sc in row).

2ND ROW: Ch 1, turn, 1 sc in each of next 120 sc.

3RD ROW: Repeat last row.

4TH ROW: Ch 1, turn, 1 sc in each of next 119 sc, change color in end sc as follows: insert hook in end st, yarn over hook, draw up a loop, pick up 2nd color and tie it to crochet as close as possible, drop 1st color, pick up 2nd color; with 2nd color, yarn over hook, draw through 2 loops of 1st color on hook to complete sc.

5TH ROW: With 2nd color, ch 2, turn, skip first sc, a hdc in next sc (yarn over hook, insert hook in next st, yarn over hook, draw up a loop, yarn over hook draw thru all 3 loops on hook for a half dc), a hdc in each remaining sc (there will be 120 hdc in row, counting ch 2 as 1 hdc).

6TH ROW: Ch 2, turn, skip first st, 1 hdc in each of next 118 sts, change color in last st as follows: yarn over, draw up a loop in top st of turning chain, drop 2nd color, pick up 1st color and with 1st color, yarn over, draw thru all 3 loops on hook of 2nd color; break off 2nd color.

7TH ROW: With 1st color, ch 1, turn, 1 sc in each st across row (120 sc in row).

8TH THROUGH 12TH ROW: Repeat last row 5 times.

13TH ROW: Ch 1, turn, 1 sc in first sc; * ch 2, skip next 2 sc, 1 sc in each of next 2 sc; repeat from * across row to 3 end sts, ch 2, skip 2 sc, 1 sc in end sc, changing to 2nd color as described in 4th row; break off 1st color.

14TH ROW: With 2nd color, ch 1, turn, 1 sc in first sc; * 2 sc in next (ch 2) space, ch 2, skip next 2 sc; repeat from * across row, end with 2 sc in last (ch 2) space, 1 sc in end sc, changing to 1st color; break off 2nd color.

15TH ROW: With 1st color, ch 1, turn, 1 sc in first sc, * ch 2, skip next 2 sc, 2 sc in next (ch 2) space; repeat from * across end with 2 sc in last (ch 2) space, ch 2, skip next 2 sc, 1 sc in end sc.

16TH ROW: Ch 1, turn, 1 sc in first sc; * 2 sc in next (ch 2) space, 1 sc in each of next 2 sc; repeat from * across row, end with 2 sc in last (ch 2) space, 1 sc in end sc.

17TH ROW: Repeat 7th row.

18TH ROW: Ch 4, turn, skip first st, 1 tr in next st as follows: (yarn over hook) twice, insert hook in next st, yarn over hook, draw up a loop, (yarn over hook, draw through 2 loops) 3 times to complete tr, 1 tr in next 117 sts, change color in last tr as follows: (yarn over hook) twice, insert hook in last st, yarn over hook, draw up a loop (yarn over hook, draw through 2 loops) twice; pick up 2nd color, tie it to crochet same as before, drop 1st color, with 2nd color, yarn over hook, draw through last 2 (1st color) loops on hook; break off 1st color.

19TH ROW: With 2nd color ch 3, turn, 1 dc in first st as follows: yarn over hook, insert hook in next st, yarn over hook, draw up a loop, (yarn over hook, draw thru 2 loops) twice to complete dc, 1 dc in next st,   * ch 3, skip next 3 sts, 1 dc in each of next 4 sts; repeat from * across row to 6 end sts, end with ch 3, skip next 3 sts, 1 dc in each of next 2 sts, 1 dc in top of turning ch 4.

20TH ROW: Ch 5, turn, skip next (3 dc) group; * 4 dc in next (ch 3) space, ch 3, skip next (4 dc) group; repeat from * across row, ending with 4 dc in last (ch 3) space, ch 2, skip next 2 dc, 1 dc in top of turning ch 3.

21ST ROW: Ch 3, turn, 2 dc in next space; * ch 3, skip next (4 dc) group, 4 dc in next space; repeat from * across row, ending with ch 3, 3 dc in end space.

22ND THROUGH 29TH ROW: Repeat 20th and 21st rows 4 more times; changing yarn to 1st color in last dc, break off 2nd color.

30TH ROW: With 1st color, ch 4, turn, skip first dc, 1 tr in each of next 3 dc, * 3 tr in next space, 1 tr in each of next 4 dc; repeat from * across row, ending with 3 tr in last space, 1 tr in each of next 2 dc (do not work in top of turning ch 3; 120 tr in row, counting beginning ch 4, as 1 tr).

31ST AND 32ND ROWS: Repeat 7th row twice.

33RD THRU 36TH ROW: Repeat 13th, 14th, 15th and 16th rows.

37TH THRU 40TH ROW: Repeat 7th row 4 times.

41ST THRU 43RD ROW: Repeat 4th, 5th and 6th rows.

44TH ROW: Ch 1, turn, a sl st (insert hook in next st, yarn over hook, draw up a loop and draw this loop thru loop on hook for a sl st), 1 sl st in each st across row (this will be the top edge of poncho and will complete First Section); break off. Make Second Section of Poncho in same manner.

BLOCKING: Pin each section to measure 14" X 30" on a padded surface; cover with a damp cloth; steam (do not press) with a warm iron. Remove when dry.

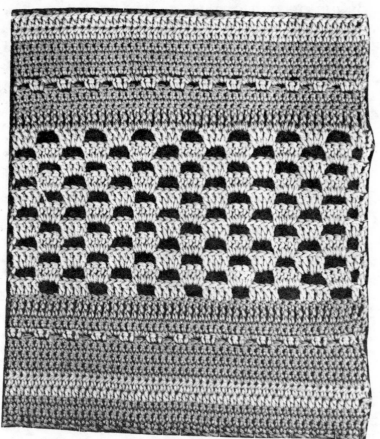

PATTERN STITCH

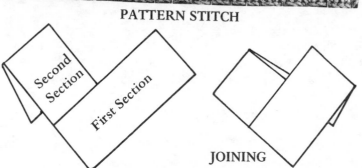

Second Section

First Section

JOINING

JOINING OF SECTIONS: Place and pin Top edge of First Section over Ends of rows of Second Section with outer edges flush (see Detail 1). Using a darning needle and matching yarn join the two sections together with back stitches. This will be the Front of Poncho. Place and pin Top edge of Second Section over <u>Ends</u> of rows of First Section (for Back of Poncho) and join in same manner as front (see Detail 2).

FRINGE — Cut a piece of cardboard 5" wide and 7" long. Wind as much yarn of both colors as needed for fringe around cardboard; cut at one end, making 14" strands. Hold 3 strands of one color together and fold them in half to form a loop; insert hook from back to front in a stitch, draw loop of strands through stitch, draw cut ends thru this loop and pull tightly to form a knot (see Details for Fringe). Alternating colors, place 3 strands (1 fringe) about 3/4" apart or, where desired along outside edges of poncho. Trim fringe evenly.

BEGINNERS' DELIGHT — THE CHIGNON CAP

MATERIALS NEEDED:

One (1 oz.) ball of Win-tot (Original chignon cap was made of it) or about 25 yards of any yarn which will give you the same gauge. A No. 6 or G Plastic Crochet Hook. 1/4 yard of round elastic.

GAUGE — WORKING IN SINGLE CROCHET
4 sts = 1 inch
9 rows = 2 inches

1ST ROUND: Make a slip loop on hook (see Page 17, Chapter 3) , *put yarn over hook from back to front, draw thru loop on hook for a chain; repeat from * 4 times for ch 5, join with a sl st into a ring by inserting hook in first chain st, yarn over hook and draw thru both stitch and loop, ch 1, 1 sc into ring (insert hook into ring under chain from front to back, yarn over hook, draw up a loop in ring (2 loops on hook), yarn over hook and thru both loops on hook for an sc); work 7 more sc into ring, end with a sl st in top of first sc of round.

2ND ROUND: Ch 3, 1 dc in same sc as sl st (yarn over hook, always insert hook from front to back under 2 top strands of sc below, yarn over hook, draw up a loop (3 loops on hook) yarn over hook, draw thru 2 loops only, yarn over hook, draw thru remaining 2 loops to complete first dc); * ch 2, 2 dc in next sc; repeat from * 6 times, end with ch 2, a sl st in top st of turning ch 3 (there will be 16 dc in round, counting first ch 3 as 1 dc).

3RD ROUND: Ch 4, 1 tr (yarn twice around hook, insert hook under 2 top strands of dc below, yarn over hook, draw up a loop (4 loops on hook), work (yarn over hook and thru 2 loops) 3 times for a tr, another tr in same dc * chain 3, 1 tr in next dc, 2 tr in next dc; repeat from * around, end with ch 3, a sl st in top st of turning ch 4 (there will be 24 tr in round counting ch 4 at beginning of round as 1 tr).

4TH ROUND: Ch 4, 1 tr in each of next 2 tr (insert hook under 2 top strands of tr below); * chain 3, 1 tr in each of next 3 tr; repeat from * around, end with ch 3, a sl st in top st of turning ch 4.

5TH ROUND: Repeat last round.

6TH ROUND: Ch 4, 1 tr in each of next 2 tr; * ch 1, 1 tr in each of next 3 tr; repeat from * around, end with ch 1, a sl st in top st of turning ch 4.

7TH ROUND: Overlap ends of 7" piece of elastic for 1/2" and sew together. Place circle of elastic along top edge of last round and working over elastic, work ch 1, 1 sc in top of turning ch, 1 sc in each of next 2 tr; * 1 sc in (ch 1) space, 1 sc in each of next 3 tr; repeat from * around, end with 1 sc in last (ch 1) space, a sl st in top of first sc. Break off.

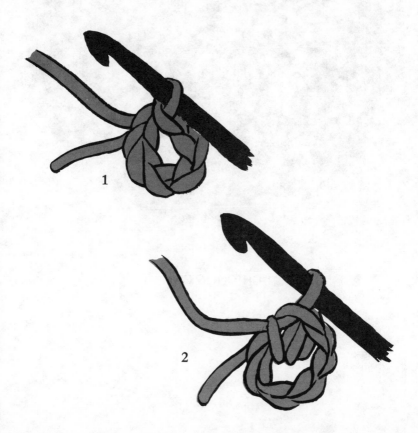

CHIGNON CAP

COVER GIRL HAT

MATERIALS NEEDED:
3 ozs. of Jiffy Wool (such as Misty, Willow Down, Speedy Knit, Opal Spun and Fluffyspun).
For Canada – 6 ozs. of Bulky.
A No. 9 or I Plastic Crochet Hook.
Original Hat was made of Misty.

GAUGE – WORKING IN SINGLE CROCHET
5 sts = 2 inches; 5 rows = 2 inches.

1ST ROUND: Ch 5, join with a sl st into a ring, ch 5, 1 tr (yarn twice around hook for a tr) into ring, (ch 1, 1 tr into ring) 14 times, ch 1, a sl st in 4th st of beginning ch 5 (there are 16 tr in round, counting the ch 4 as one tr).

2ND ROUND: Ch 5, 1 dc in next tr (ch 2, 1 dc in next tr) 14 times, ch 2, a sl st in 3rd st of beginning ch 5.

3RD ROUND: Ch 5, 1 dc in next dc (ch 2, 1 dc in next dc) 14 times, ch 2, a sl st in 3rd st of beginning ch 5.

4TH ROUND: Ch 6, 1 dc in next dc (ch 3, 1 dc in next dc) 14 times, ch 3, a sl st in 3rd st of beginning ch 6.

5TH AND 6TH ROUNDS: Repeat 4th round twice more.

7TH ROUND: Ch 1, 3 sc in next 16 (ch 3) spaces, end with a sl st in first sc of round (48 sc in round).

8TH ROUND: Ch 1, 1 sc in each of next 48 sc, end with a sl st in first sc of round.

1ST ROUND OF BRIM — Ch 1, turn, working in back strands of sts only for fold of brim, work (1 sc in each of next 5 sc, 2 sc in next sc) around, ending with a sl st in first sc of round (56 sc in round).

2ND ROUND: Ch 1, 1 sc in each of next 56 sc, end with a sl st in first sc of round.

3RD THROUGH 6TH ROUND: Repeat last round 4 times; break off.

POMPON — Cut a piece of cardboard 4-3/4" long and 5" wide; wind yarn around cardboard about 50 times. Slip a strand of yarn thru one end of loops and tie ends into a tight knot. Cut loops at opposite end. Loosen and fluff out ends by brushing them with a stiff brush. Trim ends to form a nice pompon.

Fold Brim up along ridge, then fold in half at one side (see Photograph on cover), and attach pompon.

COVER GIRL MESH SCARF

MESH SCARF (8" X 72" including fringe.)

MATERIAL REQUIREMENTS:
5 ozs of Jiffy Wool (such as Misty, Willow Down, Speedy Knit, Opal Spun and Fluffyspun).
For Canada — 5 ozs. of Bulky.
A No. 9 or I Plastic Crochet Hook.
Original scarf was made of Misty.

GAUGE — WORKING IN PATTERN STITCH
1 square mesh = 1 inch; 4 rows = 3 inches.

1ST ROW: Ch 29, (this chain should measure 9" without stretching), 1 dc in 8th st from hook; * ch 2, skip next 2 sts, 1 dc in next st; repeat from * across chain, ending with ch 2, skip 2 sts, 1 dc in end st (there are 8 square meshes in row).

2ND ROW: Ch 5, turn, skip first dc, 1 dc in next dc; * ch 2, 1 dc in next dc; repeat from * across row, ending with ch 2, skip 2 sts of turning chain, 1 dc in next ch st.
Repeat 2nd Row until scarf measures about 60 inches, which allows 2" for Blocking and 10 inches for fringe; break off.

BLOCKING: Pin scarf to measure 8" X 62" on a padded surface; cover with a damp cloth; steam (do not press) with a warm iron. Remove when dry.

FRINGE: Wind a single strand of yarn 3 times around a 6-1/2 inch piece of cardboard. Cut at one end, thus making 13-inch strands. Hold these strands together and fold in half to make a loop; insert hook, from back to front, in first stitch of foundation chain of scarf and draw loop of strands through, draw loose ends through this loop and pull tightly to form a knot. Cut and tie a group of strands in same manner in every space across end of scarf. Tie fringe across opposite end in same manner. Trim all fringe evenly. (See Pg. 46 for details on fringe.)

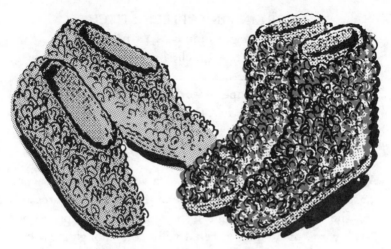

LOOPY SLIPPERS OR BOOTS

Yarns in Parentheses (   ) are Canadian yarns.

MATERIALS NEEDED AND SIZES

Style	Size	Material	Quantity	Crochet Hook
Slipper	Small Medium Large	Sport Yarn or (4-ply Fingering Yarn)	4 ozs. main color 2 ozs. contrasting color	No. 6 or G Plastic
Boot	Small Medium Large	Sport Yarn or (4-ply Fingering Yarn)	6 ozs. main color 2 ozs. contrasting color	

2/3 yard of narrow velvet ribbon required for boot. 120 yards of rug cotton or rag strips (3/4 inch wide) will make a pair of crocheted soles.

WORKING IN PATTERN STITCH
(Using 2 strands of Yarn)
GAUGE   3 sts = 1 inch; 4 rounds = 1 inch

NOTE: Upper of slipper is worked entirely with 2 strands
of yarn held together. Do not use a single strand.

RAG STRIPS FOR CROCHETED SOLES

Any lightweight cotton material or a very cheap unbleached
muslin can be used for making the rag strips. If the material is
not the desired color, tint it before tearing strips. About
2-1/2 yards of 36-inch material will make enough rags for a
pair of soles. Tear the strips lengthwise, making them 3/4
inch wide. It is not necessary to join all the rag strips together
as the joining can be made as the crochet is being done. When
the end of the strip is reached, overlap the end of new strip
over the end of finished strip about 1 inch.

Follow directions for crocheted soles below.

CROCHETED SOLES
(FOR ALL SIZES)
Small Size: 3-1/2 X 9 Inches;
Medium Size: 3-1/2 X 10 Inches;
Large Size: 3-1/2 X 10-3/4 Inches.

TOP SECTION—1ST ROW: With rug cotton or rags ch 6, 1 sc
in 2nd st from hook, 1 sc in each of remaining 4 sts of
chain.

2ND ROW: Ch 1, turn, 2 sc in first sc of last row (this forms
an increase at beginning of row), 1 sc in each of remaining
sc.

3RD ROW: Same as last row.

4TH ROW: Ch 1, turn, 1 sc in each sc of last row.

Repeat last row 10 times for small size (12 times for medium size or 14 times for large size); there are 7 sc in each row.

Repeat 2nd row twice.

*Work a row even, increase a st at beginning of next row; repeat from * once; there are 11 sc in last row.

Repeat 4th row (even row) 6 times for small size (8 times for medium size or 10 times for large size); there are 11 sc in each row.

1ST DECREASING ROW: Ch 1, turn, skip first 2 sc, 1 sc in each of remaining sc.

Repeat last row 3 times.

BORDER ROUND: Ch 1, do not turn, working along end of rows work 1 sc over end st of each row to foundation ch, 1 sc in each st of chain, 1 sc over opposite end st of each row, 1 sc in each st across last row, a sl st in first sc of round; break off.

BOTTOM SECTION: Same as Top Section.

JOINING OF SECTIONS: Place top section over bottom section, matching edges. With a darning needle and very strong sewing thread, sew sections together with small running stitches.

Make a duplicate sole.

UPPER FOR BOOT
(FOR ALL SIZES)

TOP SECTION—1ST ROW: Using 2 strands of yarn in main color held together, ch 30 loosely for small size (ch 34 for medium size or ch 38 for large size), 1 sc in 2nd st from hook, 1 sc in each of remaining sts of chain (there are 29 sc for small size, 33 for medium size or 37 for large size).

2ND ROW: Ch 1, turn, 2 sc in first sc of last row, 1 sc in each sc to end sc, 2 sc in end sc (there are 31 sc for small size, 35 for medium size or 39 for large size).

3RD ROW: Ch 1, turn, 1 sc in each sc of last row; break off 1 strand of yarn, tie contrasting color to end sc.

4TH ROW: With two colors ch 1, turn, work a loop st in first sc as follows: cut a piece of cardboard 1-1/2 inches wide and about 3 inches long, hold cardboard in back of work (see Detail 1); insert hook in first sc, wind double yarn around cardboard from back to front (see Detail 2); yarn over hook, draw up a loop through st on hook (see Detail 2); yarn over, draw through 2 loops on hook (see Detail 3); work a loop st in each sc of last row (there are 31 loop sts on small size, 35 on medium size or 39 on large size).

5TH ROW: Ch 1, turn, 1 sc in first loop st of last row, 1 sc in each of remaining loop sts.

6TH ROW: Ch 1, turn, a loop st in first sc of last row, a loop st in each of remaining sc.

Repeat 5th and 6th rows once; repeat 5th row once more.

10TH ROW: Ch 1, turn, 2 loop sts in first sc of last row, a loop st in each of next 29 sc for small size (33 sc for medium size or 37 sc for large size), 2 loop sts in end sc, join with a sl st in first loop st at beginning of row being careful not to twist work.

1ST ROUND: Ch 1, 1 sc in same st as last sl st, 1 sc in each of remaining sts, a sl st in first sc of round (there are 33 sc for small size, 37 sc for medium size or 41 sc for large size).

2ND ROUND: Ch 1, a loop st in same st as last sl st, a loop st in each of remaining sts, a sl st in first loop st of round.

Repeat 1st and 2nd rounds 3 more times.

9TH ROUND: Ch 1, 1 sc in same st as last sl st, *1 sc in each of next 3 sts, 2 sc in next st; repeat from * around, a sl st in first sc of round (there are 41 sc for small size, 46 for medium size or 51 for large size).

10TH ROUND: Same as 2nd round.

11TH ROUND: Ch 1, 1 sc in same st as last sl st, 1 sc in each of remaining sts, a sl st in first sc of round.

12TH ROUND: Same as 2nd round; break off.

FRONT SECTION—1ST ROW: Holding loop side of work toward you, skip first 15 sts of last round (17 sts for medium size or 19 sts for large size), join yarn with a sl st in next st, ch 1, 1 sc in each of next 9 sts for small size (11 sts for medium size or 13 sts for large size); do not work over remaining sts.

2ND ROW: Ch 1, turn, a loop st in each sc of last row.

3RD ROW: Ch 1, turn, 1 sc in each loop st of last row.

Repeat 2nd and 3rd rows of Front Section 2 more times for small and medium sizes (or 3 more times for large size); repeat 2nd row once more.

1ST DECREASING ROW: Ch 1, turn, work a 2-joined sc over first 2 sts of last row as follows: draw up a loop in each of first 2 sts, yarn over hook, draw thru all 3 loops on hook, 1 sc in all but last 2 loop sts, work a 2-joined sc over end 2 sts.

NEXT ROW: Ch 1, turn, a loop st in 2-joined sc, a loop st in each st across row.

Repeat last 2 rows until 3 loop sts remain.

LAST ROW: Ch 1, turn, draw up a loop in each of 3 sts of last row, yarn over hook, draw loop thru all 4 loops on hook, ch 1; break off.

13TH ROUND: Holding right side of work toward you and using 2 strands of main color, join yarn with a sl st in same st as end sl st of 12th round; ch 1, 1 sc in same st as joining sl st, skip sl st, 1 sc in each st of last round to Front Section, 1 sc over end st of each of next 15 rows for small size (17 rows for medium size or 21 rows for large size) of Front Section, 1 sc in 3-joined sc, 1 sc over end st of each row at opposite side of Front Section, 1 sc in each remaining st of last round (62 sc in round for small size, 69 sc for medium size or 80 sc for large size), a sl st in first sc of round.

14TH ROUND: Ch 1, 1 sc in same sc as sl st, 1 sc in each of remaining sc, a sl st in first sc of round.

Repeat last round once; break off.

TOP EDGE: Holding right side of work toward you and using 2 strands of main color, join yarn with a sl st in first st of foundation ch; ch 1, 3 sc in same st as sl st, 1 sc in each st of foundation ch to end st, 3 sc in end st, 1 sc over each end st of next 10 rows, working along opposite end sts of rows work 1 sc over each of next 10 rows, a sl st in first sc of round; break off.

BOW: Cut velvet ribbon into two 12-inch pieces, fold over edge 1/2 inch and sew to each corner of top edging.

JOINING TO SOLE: Using a darning needle and same yarn, overcast bottom edge of upper securely to outer edge of sole being careful to have center front of upper to center of toe of sole and center back to center of foundation ch of sole.

Make other slipper in same way.

UPPER FOR SLIPPER
(FOR ALL SIZES)

TOP SECTION —1ST ROUND: Using 2 strands of yarn in main color held together, ch 33 loosely for small size (ch 37 for medium size or ch 41 for large size), join with a sl st to first st of chain (thus forming a circle being careful not to twist sts (this chain should slip easily over foot), ch 1, 1 sc in same st as sl st, 1 sc in each of remaining sts of chain, a sl st in first sc at beginning of round (there are 33 sc for small size, 37 for medium size or 41 for large size).

2ND ROUND: Ch 1, 1 sc in same st as last sl st, 1 sc in each of remaining sc, a sl st in first sc of round; break off one strand of yarn tie contrasting color to end sc.

3RD ROUND: With 2 colors ch 1, work a loop st in same st as last sl st as follows: cut a piece of cardboard 1-1/2 inches wide and about 3 inches long, hold cardboard in back of work (see Detail 1); insert hook in same st as last sl st, wind double yarn around cardboard from back to front (see Detail 2); yarn over hook, draw up a loop through st on hook (see Detail 2); yarn over, draw thru 2 loops on hook (see Detail 3); work a loop st in each of next 32 sc of last row (there are 37 loop sts for medium size or 41 loop sts for large size), a sl st in first loop st of round.

4TH ROUND: Ch 1, 1 sc in same st as last sl st, 1 sc in each of remaining sc, a sl st in first sc of round.

Repeat 3rd and 4th rounds 3 times; repeat 3rd round once more; break off.

Follow directions for Boot from Front Section to Top edge.

JOINING TO SOLE: Same as for Boot.

Make other slipper in same way.

PATTERN STITCH

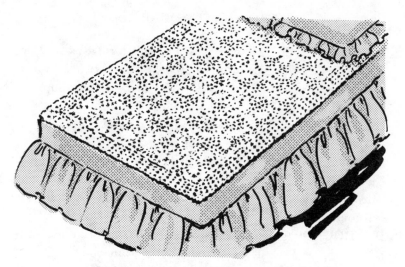

BEDSPREAD OF LACY SQUARES

MATERIALS NEEDED AND SIZES

Original bedspread crocheted of Phentex Knitting Yarn of 100% Celaspun in 3-1/2 oz. balls.
A No. 8 or H Plastic Crochet Hook is required.
EACH (12 inch) SQUARE TAKES ABOUT 100 yds.

BEDSPREAD

Size	Single 46-1/2″ X 85-1/2″	Double 59-1/2″ X 85-1/2″
Material Needed	16 balls	20 balls
No. of Squares	18	24
Squares in Rows	6	6
No. of Rows	3	4

CROCHETED SQUARE

1ST ROUND: Ch 4, join with a sl st into a ring, ch 3, 2 dc into ring, *ch 3, 3 dc into ring; repeat from * twice, ch 3, a sl st in top st of first ch 3 (there are 4-3 dc groups in round).

2ND ROUND: A sl st in each of first 2 dc, a sl st in next (ch 3) loop, ch 3, 2 dc in same ch loop as last sl st, (ch 2, 3 dc in same ch loop as last dc) twice, *skip next 3 dc, (3 dc, ch 2, 3 dc, ch 2 and 3 dc) all in next (ch 3) loop; repeat from * twice, a sl st in top st of first ch 3 at beginning of round.

3RD ROUND: A sl st in each of first 2 dc, a sl st in next (ch 2) loop, ch 3, (2 dc, ch 2 and 3 dc) in same ch loop as last sl st, *ch 3, skip next 3 dc, work a shell of (3 dc, ch 2 and 3 dc) in next ch loop, skip next 3 dc, a shell in next (ch 2) loop; repeat from * around, end with ch 3, skip next 3 dc, a shell in next (ch 2) loop, a slip st in top st of first ch 3 at beginning of round.

4TH ROUND: A sl st in each of first 2 dc, a sl st in next (ch 2) loop, ch 3, (2 dc, ch 2 and 3 dc) in same ch loop as last sl st, *ch 2, 6 dc in center st of next (ch 3) loop, ch 2, always working shell in (ch 2) loop of shell below, work a shell in each of next 2 shells; repeat from * around, end with ch 2, 6 dc in center st of next (ch 3) loop, ch 2, a shell in next shell, a sl st in top st of first ch 3 at beginning of round.

5TH ROUND: A sl st in each of first 2 dc, a sl st in next (ch 2) loop, ch 3, (2 dc, ch 2 and 3 dc) in same ch loop as last sl st, *ch 3, skip next (ch 2) loop, 1 sc in next dc, (ch 3 and 1 sc) in each of next 5 dc, ch 3, a shell in shell, ch 4, a shell in next shell; repeat from * around, end with ch 4, a sl st in top st of first ch 3 at beginning of round.

6TH ROUND: A sl st in each of first 2 dc, a sl st in next (ch 2) loop, ch 3, (2 dc, ch 2 and 3 dc) in same ch loop as last sl st, *ch 3, skip next (ch 3) loop, 1 sc in next (ch 3) loop, (ch 3 and 1 sc) in each of next 4 ch loops, ch 3, a shell in next shell, ch 4, 1 dc in next (ch 4) space, ch 4, a shell in next shell; repeat from * around, end with ch 4, a sl st in top st of first ch 3 at beginning of round.

7TH ROUND: A sl st in each of next 2 dc, a sl st in next (ch 2) loop, ch 3, (2 dc, ch 2 and 3 dc) in same ch loop as last sl st, *ch 3, skip next (ch 3) loop, 1 sc in next (ch 3) loop, (ch 3 and 1 sc) in each of next 3 ch loops, ch 3, a shell in next shell, (ch 4, 1 dc in next ch 4 space) twice, ch 4, a shell in next shell; repeat from * around, end with ch 4 a sl st in top st of first ch 3 at beginning of round.

FIRST CORNER—1ST ROW: A sl st in each of first 2 dc, a sl st in next (ch 2) loop, ch 3, (2 dc, ch 2 and 3 dc) in same ch loop as last sl st, ch 3, skip next (ch 3) loop, 1 sc in next (ch 3) loop, (ch 3 and 1 sc) in each of next 2 ch loops, ch 3, a shell in next shell; do not work over remaining sts.

2ND ROW: Turn, a sl st in each of first 3 dc, a sl st in next (ch 2) loop, ch 3, (2 dc, ch 2 and 3 dc) in same ch loop as last sl st, ch 3, skip a ch loop, 1 sc in next ch loop, ch 3, 1 sc in next ch loop, ch 3, a shell in end shell.

3RD ROW: Turn, a sl st in each of first 3 dc, a sl st in next (ch 2) loop, ch 3, (2 dc, ch 2 and 3 dc) in same ch loop as last sl st, ch 3, skip a ch loop, 1 sc in next ch loop, ch 3, a shell in end shell.

4TH ROW: Turn, a sl st in each of first 3 dc, a sl st in next (ch 2) loop, ch 3, (2 dc, ch 2 and 3 dc) in same ch loop as last sl st, skip next 2 (ch 3) loops, 3 dc in (ch 2) loop of next shell, ch 1, turn, a sl st in (ch 2) loop of last shell made, ch 1, turn, 3 dc in same (ch 2) loop as last dc; break off.

SECOND CORNER—1ST ROW: Turn, skip next 3 (ch 4) loops of last round, join yarn with a sl st in (ch 2) loop of next shell, ch 3, (2 dc, ch 2 and 3 dc) in same ch loop as last sl st, ch 3, skip next (ch 3) loop, 1 sc in next (ch 3) loop, (ch 3 and 1 sc) in each of next 2 ch loops, ch 3, a shell in next shell; do not work over remaining sts.
Now follow directions for 2nd, 3rd and 4th rows of First Corner.

THIRD AND FOURTH CORNERS: Follow directions for Second Corner.
Make 17 more squares for Single Size Bedspread, 23 more squares for Double Size Bedspread.

SMALL MEDALLIONS: Ch 3, join with a sl st into a ring, ch 1, *1 sc into ring, ch 5; repeat from * 3 times, a sl st in first sc of round; break off.
Make 9 more Small Medallions for Single Size Bedspread, 14 more Small Medallions for Double Size Bedspread.

BLOCKING: SEE PAGE 41

JOINING OF SQUARES: Using a sewing needle and heavy duty sewing thread, fasten thread to a corner shell on first square (see A on Illustration of Square; fasten to corresponding shell on second square; break off. Tack each of next 3 shells marked B, C and D to corresponding shells on second square; break off after each joining. Skip next space, tack next space from E to F to corresponding space on second square; break off. Tack each of next 4 shells marked G, H, I, and J, to corresponding shells on second square.

The squares are joined in rows; then the rows are joined together.

JOINING OF SMALL MEDALLIONS: Place a small medallion in center of 4 joined squares. Tack center st of (ch 5) loop of small medallion to end st of a corner shell; break off. Tack remaining 3 (ch 5) loops to remaining end sts of 3 corner shells; break off after each joining.

A B C D   E F   G H I J

EDGING—1ST ROUND: Holding right side of work toward you, join yarn with an sc in top of corner shell of corner square (see P on Detail of Joined Squares), *(ch 3, 1 sc in top of end st of shell of next row) 3 times, ch 6, skip next (ch 4) space, 5 sc in next space, ch 6, skip next (ch 4) space, 1 sc in top of end st of 1st row of corner, (ch 3, 1 sc in top of end st of next row) 3 times, ch 3, a 2 joined dc in (ch 2) loop of joined shell of same square and next square as follows: Yarn over hook, draw up a loop in (ch 2) loop of joined shells, yarn over hook and through 2 loops, yarn over hook, draw up a loop in (ch 2) loop of joined shells on next square, yarn over hook and thru 2 loops, yarn over hook thru all 3 loops on hook, ch 3, 1 sc in top of end st of next shell of first row of corner; repeat from * to corner square, (ch 3, 1 sc in top of end st of shell of next row) 3 times, ch 6, skip next (ch 4) space, 5 sc in next space, ch 6, skip next (ch 4) space, 1 sc in top of end st of 1st row of corner, (ch 3, 1 sc in top of end st of next row) 3 times, ch 7, 1 sc in top of end st of same row as last sc; repeat from first * around, but do not work last sc, instead end with a sl st in first sc of round.

2ND ROUND: Ch 1, 1 sc in same sc as last sl st, *a shell in next sc, 1 sc in next sc, a shell in next sc, 1 sc in next (ch 6) loop, a shell in next sc, skip next sc, 1 sc in next sc, skip next sc, a shell in next sc, 1 sc in next (ch 6) loop, (a shell in next sc, 1 sc in next sc) twice, a shell in 2 joined dc, 1 sc in next sc; repeat from * across to corner square, a shell in next sc, 1 sc in next sc, a shell in next sc, 1 sc in next (ch 6) loop, a shell in next sc, skip next sc, 1 sc in next sc, skip next sc, a shell in next sc, 1 sc in next (ch 6 loop, (a shell in next sc, 1 sc in next sc) twice, (a shell, 1 sc, 3 dc, ch 3, 3 dc, 1 sc and a shell) all in corner (ch 7) loop, 1 sc in next sc; repeat from first * around, but do not work last sc, instead end with a sl st in first sc of round.

3RD ROUND: A sl st in each of next 3 dc, a sl st in next (ch 2) loop, ch 3, (2 dc, ch 2 and 3 dc) in same (ch 2) loop as last sl st, *(skip next sc, a shell in next shell) to (ch 3) loop of corner group, work (3 dc, ch 2, 3 dc, ch 2, 3 dc, ch 2 and 3 dc) all in (ch 3) loop; repeat from * around, end with a sl st in top st of first ch 3.

4TH ROUND: A sl st in each of next 2 dc, a sl st in next (ch 2) loop, ch 3, (2 dc, ch 2 and 3 dc) in same (ch 2) loop as last sl st, *a shell in next (ch 2) loop; repeat from * around, end with a sl st in top st of first ch 3.

5TH ROUND: A sl st in each of next 2 dc, a sl st in next (ch 2) loop, ch 3, (2 dc, ch 2 and 3 dc) in same (ch 2) loop as last sl st, (a shell in each shell to corner shell, (3 dc, ch 2, 3 dc, ch 2, 3 dc, ch 2 and 3 dc) all in corner shell; repeat from * around, end with a sl st in top st of first ch 3 at beginning of round; break off.

JOINING OF LACY SQUARES

RUFFLED SPREAD

MATERIALS NEEDED: Cotton Broadcloth, Polished Cotton or Synthetic Mixtures 42/45 inches wide.

FOR SINGLE AND, DOUBLE SIZE BEDSPREAD: Top of bed requires 2-1/4 yds. material for single size bed (4-1/2 yds. material for double size bed).

To determine amount of yardage for ruffle measure bed from top of mattress to floor, take off 8 inches for band around top of ruffle, add 3 inches for hem and seam allowances; this measurement should be multiplied by 10 for single bed size (11 for double bed size). There are 4 strips for each side, 2 for front for single size or 3 for double size bed. Divide last figure by 36 inches which will give you the amount needed for ruffle. For border above ruffle you will need 5 — 9" strips for single or double size spread. For each pillow you will need 2 yds. of material.

CUTTING DIRECTIONS—FOR SINGLE BED: For top of bed cut material 40 X 77 Inches.

Cut 10 strips for ruffle Cut 5 — 9" strips for border.

FOR SHOW-PILLOW: Cut one piece 19 X 25 inches for top of pillow; for underside cut 2 pieces 19 X 14 inches. Cut 4 pieces 6 X 42 inches.

FOR DOUBLE BED: For top of bed cut center piece 42 X 77 inches, cut 2 strips 7-1/2 X 77 inches. Cut 11 strips for ruffle. FOR TWO PILLOWS: Cut two pieces 19 X 25 inches for top of pillow; for the underside cut 4 pieces 19 X 14 inches. Cut 5 pieces 6 X 42 inches, from material left over from top of spread cut 3 pieces 6 X 77 inches.

SEWING DIRECTIONS—(ALL SEAM ALLOWANCES 1/2 INCH)

FOR DOUBLE BED ONLY: Sew 7-1/2 inch strips to each side of center strip.

FOR BOTH SIZES: Sew 5 border strips together along short sides. Sew these 5 strips along 2 long and 1 short side of top for bed, cut excess away from border strip. Sew a half inch hem along other side. Sew 10 pieces together along short side of ruffle for bed for single size (11 pieces for double size). Sew a half inch seam on each short side of ruffle. Sew a 2 inch hem on one edge plus 1/2 inch for turn under. Gather top side of ruffle to fit around edge of border (about 187 inches for single size, about 204 inches for double bed). Sew ruffle to edge of border.

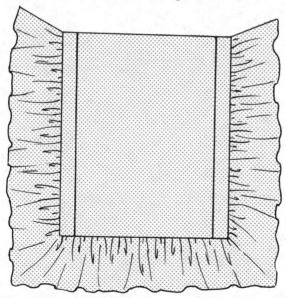

FINISHING—Stitch crochet piece to top of spread.

FOR PILLOW: Sew short side of strips for ruffle together making 1/2 inch seams. (For double bed, cut joined strips in half—224 inches for each pillow). Sew short side of pieces together. Fold pieces in half lengthwise, stitch open edges together. Ruffle piece to measure 84 inches. Sew ruffle around front section of pillow. Sew 1/2 inch hem on one 19" edge on each underside piece. Place hemmed side of pieces 4 inches over one another and stitch in place. Sew underside to top section of pillow; turn right side out. Slip in your pillows.

MOTHER AND DAUGHTER SKIRTS

MATERIAL NEEDED AND SIZES

Skirt	Size	Material	Quantity	Crochet Hook
Misses	10-12	4-ply Knitting Worsted	12 ozs.	No. 8 or H Plastic
Misses	14-16	4-ply Knitting Worsted	14 ozs.	No. 8 or H Plastic
Girls	2-4	4-ply Knitting Worsted	4 ozs.	No. 8 or H Plastic
Girls	6-8	4-ply Knitting Worsted	6 ozs.	No. 8 or H Plastic
Girls	10-12	4-ply Knitting Worsted	7 ozs.	No. 8 or H Plastic

GAUGE FOR FIRST 5 ROUNDS
3 shells = 3-1/2 inches;
2 rounds = 1 inch.

CHILD'S SKIRT
(FOR ALL SIZES)

FOUNDATION CHAIN: Starting at waist ch 90 for Size 2-4 (ch 100 for Size 6-8; ch 110 for Size 10-12); this chain should measure, without stretching, 22 inches for Size 2-4 (24 inches for Size 6-8; 26 inches for Size 10-12); being careful not to twist chain, join with a sl st in first st of chain to form a circle.

CAUTION: CIRCLE OF CHAIN SHOULD STRETCH TO SLIP OVER CHILD'S HEAD AND SHOULDERS.

1ST ROUND: Ch 1, 1 sc in same st as sl st, *skip next st, a shell of 3 dc in next st, skip next 2 sts, 1 sc in next st; repeat from * around, ending with skip next st, a shell of 3 dc in next st, skip last 2 sts, a sl st in first sc at beginning of round. There are 18 shells in round for Size 2-4 (20 for Size 6-8; 22 for Size 10-12).

2ND ROUND: Ch 3, 1 dc in same sc as sl st, 1 sc in center dc of next shell, *skip next dc, 3 dc in next sc, 1 sc in center dc of next shell; repeat from * around, ending with 1 dc in same sc as first dc of this round, a sl st in top st of ch 3 at beginning of round.

3RD ROUND: Ch 1, 1 sc in same st as sl st, *skip next dc, 3 dc in next sc, 1 sc in center dc of next shell; repeat from * around, ending with 3 dc in last sc, a sl st in first sc of round. Each round has same number of shells as first round throughout skirt.

4TH AND 5TH ROUNDS: Repeat 2nd and 3rd rounds.

6TH ROUND: Ch 3, 1 dc in same st as last sl st, 1 sc in center dc of next shell, *a shell of 4 dc in next sc between shells, 1 sc in center dc of next shell, 3 dc in next sc between shells, 1 sc in center dc of next shell; repeat from * around, ending last repeat with 1 dc in same st as first dc of round, a sl st in top st of ch-3 at beginning of round.

7TH ROUND: CH 1, 1 sc in same st as last sl st, *4 dc in next sc between shells, 1 sc in 2nd dc of next shell; repeat from * around, ending with 4 dc in last sc, a sl st in first sc of round.

8TH ROUND: Ch 3, 1 dc in same st as last sl st, *1 sc in 3rd dc of next shell, 4 dc in next sc; repeat from * around, ending with 2 dc in same st as first dc of round, a sl st in top st of ch-3.

9TH ROUND: Ch 1, 1 sc in same st as last sl st, *4 dc in next sc, 1 sc in 3rd dc of next shell; repeat from * around ending with 4 dc in last sc, a sl st in first sc of round.

10TH THROUGH 13TH ROUNDS: Repeat 8th and 9th rounds, twice.

14TH ROUND: Ch 3, 2 dc in same st as last sl st, *1 sc in 3rd dc of next shell, a shell of 5 dc in next sc between shells; repeat from * around, ending with 1 sc in 3rd dc of last shell, 2 dc in same st as first dc, a sl st in top st of Ch 3.

15TH ROUND: Ch 1, 1 sc in same st as last sl st, *5 dc in next sc, 1 sc in center dc of next shell; repeat from * around, ending with 5 dc in last sc, a sl st in first sc of round.

Repeat 14th and 15th rounds twice for Size 2 (3 times for Size 4; 5 times for Size 6; 7 times for Size 8; 10 times for Size 10; 11 times for Size 12); or until skirt is the desired length, allowing about 1 inch for stretching when blocking. At end of last round, break off.

TOP EDGING—1ST ROUND: From right side, working along opposite side of foundation chain, join yarn with 1 sc in space between first sc and next shell of first round, 1 more sc in same space, *2 sc in next space between shell and next sc, 2 sc in next space between sc and next shell; repeat from * around, ending with a sl st in first sc of round.

2ND ROUND: Ch 1, 1 sc in same sc as last sl st, 1 sc in each sc around, a sl st in first sc of round. There are 72 sc in round for Size 2-4 (80 for Size 6-8; 88 for Size 10-12); (96 sts in round for Ladies' Size 10-12; 108 sc for Size 14-16).

CASING: With wrong side of skirt toward you, join yarn with 1 sc in the two loops at base of first sc of last round of edging, *ch 3, skip 1/2-inch to the left, work 1 sc at base of a st on 2nd round of skirt, ch 3, skip 1/2-inch, work 1 sc at base of next sc on 2nd round of edging; repeat from * around, ending with ch 3, a sl st in first sc of round; break off.

BLOCKING: Pin skirt to the correct size and shape on a padded surface; cover with a damp cloth; steam lightly with a warm iron. Remove when dry. Steam out folds.

FINISHING: Cut the (1/2-inch wide) elastic same length as desired waist measurement. Insert inside casing, overlap ends for 1 inch and sew together.

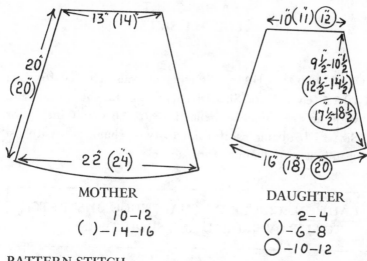

MOTHER

10-12
( )-14-16

DAUGHTER

2-4
( )-6-8
◯-10-12

PATTERN STITCH

LADIES SKIRT
(FOR ALL SIZES)

FOUNDATION CHAIN: Starting at waist ch 120 for Size 10-12 (ch 130 for Size 14-16); this chain should measure without stretching 28 inches for Size 10-12; 30 inches for Size 14-16; being careful not to twist chain, join with a sl st in first st of chain to form a circle.

CAUTION: CIRCLE OF CHAIN SHOULD STRETCH TO SLIP OVER HEAD AND SHOULDERS

1ST ROUND: Same as 1st round for Child's Skirt. There are 24 shells for Size 10-12; 26 shells for Size 14-16.
Now follow directions for Child's Skirt from 2nd round to end of 9th round.
10TH THROUGH 17TH ROUNDS: Repeat 8th and 9th rounds 4 times.
19TH AND 20TH ROUNDS: Same as 14th and 15th rounds for Child's Skirt.

NOTE: Skirt is 20 inches long when completed, if a shorter or longer skirt is desired, work less or more rounds of the next 2 rounds, allowing 2 rounds to the inch.
Repeat 14th and 15th rounds 10 times (or desired length); break off.
Now follow directions for Child's Skirt from Top Edging to end.

MOTHER & DAUGHTER VESTS

Yarns in parentheses ( ) are Canadian yarns.
Original garment made of Soufflé; which comes in 1-3/4
oz. balls.

MATERIALS NEEDED AND SIZES

Article	Size	Material Needed	Quantity	Crochet Hook
(Vest) For Mother	10-12	Soufflé	4 balls	No. 8 or H Plastic
		(Berella Sportspun)	8 ozs.	
		4-ply Knitting Worsted	12 ozs.	
	14-16	Soufflé	5 balls	
		(Berella Sportspun	10 ozs.	
		4-ply Knitting Worsted	14 ozs.	
(Vest) For Daughter	2-4	Soufflé	2 balls	
		(Berella Sportspun	4 ozs.	
		4-ply Knitting Worsted	5 ozs.	
	6-8	Soufflé	3 balls	
		(Berella Sportspun)	6 ozs.	
		4-ply Knitting Worsted	7 ozs.	
	10-12	Soufflé	3 balls	
		(Berella Sportspun)	6 ozs.	
		4-ply Knitting Worsted	9 ozs.	

GAUGE   WORKING IN PATTERN STITCH

3 (ch-2) spaces = 2 inches;
5 rows = 3 inches.

VEST
(FOR MOTHER'S SIZES)

BACK—1ST ROW: Ch 86 for Size 10-12 (ch 95 for Size 14-16); this chain should measure, without stretching, 19 inches for Size 10-12 (21 inches for Size 14-16); 1 dc in 8th st from hook, *ch 2, skip next 2 sts, 1 dc in next st; repeat from * across chain. There are 27 spaces in row for Size 10-12 (30 spaces for Size 14-16).

2ND ROW: Ch 5, turn, skip first dc, 1 dc in next dc, *ch 2, 1 dc in next dc; repeat from * across row, ending with ch 2, 1 dc in 3rd st of turning chain (there are as many spaces as in last row).

Last row forms pattern stitch.

Repeat 2nd row 27 more times for Size 10-12 (29 more times for Size 14-16).

ARMHOLES—1ST ROW: Turn, a sl st in each of first 10 sts, ch 4, 1 dc in next dc, *ch 2, 1 dc in next dc; repeat from * across to within last 4 spaces, ch 1, 1 dc in next dc; do not work over remaining spaces.

2ND ROW: Ch 4, turn, skip first dc, 1 dc in next dc, *ch 2, 1 dc in next dc, ch 1, 1 dc in next dc; repeat from * across row to within last space, ch 1, 1 dc in 2nd ch st of end space.

3RD ROW: Ch 4, turn, skip first dc, 1 dc in next dc, *ch 1, 1 dc in next dc; repeat from * across row, ending with ch 1, 1 dc in 2nd ch st of turning ch. There are 21 spaces for Size 10-12 (24 spaces for Size 14-16).

4TH ROW: Ch 3, turn, skip first dc, 1 dc in next dc, work (ch 1 and 1 dc) in each dc across to turning chain, (do not ch 1), 1 dc in 2nd st of turning chain.

5TH ROW: Ch 4, turn, skip first 2 dc, 1 dc in next dc, work (ch 1 and 1 dc) in each dc across row; do not work over turning ch. There are 19 spaces in row for Size 10-12 (23 for Size 14-16).

6TH, 7TH AND 8TH ROWS: Repeat 3rd, 4th and 5th rows of Armholes. There are 17 spaces for Size 10-12 (20 for Size 14-16).

Now repeat 3rd row of Armholes 3 times for Size 10-12 (5 times for Size 14-16).

SHOULDERS—NEXT ROW: Ch 1, turn, a sl st in first dc, work (ch 1 and 1 sc) in each of next 2 dc, ch 1, yarn over hook, draw up a loop in next dc, yarn over hook and draw through all 3 loops on hook (this forms a hdc), ch 1, 1 hdc in next dc, (ch 1 and 1 dc) in each of the next 2 dc for Size 10-12 (in each of 3 dc for Size 14-16); break off. Skip next 5 spaces for Size 10-12 (6 spaces for Size 14-16); join yarn with a sl st in next dc, ch 4, 1 dc in next dc, For Size 14-16 Only: ch 1, 1 dc in next dc; For All Sizes: (ch 1 and 1 hdc) in each of next 2dc, (ch 1 and 1 sc) in each of next 2 dc, ch 1, a sl st in 2nd ch st of turning ch; break off.

LEFT FRONT—1ST ROW: Ch 41 for Size 10-12 (ch 47 for Size 14-16); this chain should measure 9 inches for Size 10-12 (10-1/2 inches for Size 14-16); work same as 1st row of Back. There are 12 spaces in row for Size 10-12 (14 spaces for Size 14-16).

2ND ROW: Repeat 2nd row of Back.

Repeat 2nd row 27 more times for Size 10-12 (29 more times for Size 14-16).

ARMHOLE—1ST ROW: Turn, a sl st in each of first 10 sts, ch 4, 1 dc in next dc, *ch 2, 1 dc in next dc; repeat from * across row, ending with ch 2, 1 dc in 3rd st of turning chain. There are 9 spaces in row for Size 10-12 (11 for Size 14-16).

2ND ROW: Ch 4, turn, skip first dc, 1 dc in next dc, *ch 2, 1 dc in next dc, ch 1, 1 dc in next dc; repeat from * across row to within last space, ch 1, 1 dc in 2nd ch st of end space.

3RD ROW: Same as 3rd row of Back Armholes.

4TH ROW: CH 4, turn, skip first dc, 1 dc in next dc, (ch 1 and 1 dc) in each dc across row to turning ch; (do not ch 1), 1 dc in 2nd ch st of turning ch.

5TH ROW: Ch 4, turn, skip first 2 dc, 1 dc in next dc, (ch 1 and 1 dc) in each dc across row, ending with ch 1, 1 dc in 2nd ch st of turning ch. There are 8 spaces in row for Size 10-12 (10 spaces for Size 14-16).

6TH ROW: CH 4, turn, skip first dc, 1 dc in next dc, (ch 1 and 1 dc) in each dc across row, ending with ch 1, 1 dc in 2nd st of turning ch.

Repeat last 4 rows (3rd through 6th rows) once for Size 10-12 (twice for Size 14-16).

There are 7 spaces in last row for Size 10-12 (8 spaces for Size 14-16). Now repeat 6th row of Armhole once for Size 10-12 (3 times for Size 14-16); last row should end at front edge.

SHOULDER—NEXT ROW: Ch 3, turn, skip first dc, 1 dc in next dc, (ch 1 and 1 dc) in next dc for Size 10-12 (in each of 2 dc for Size 14-16), work (ch 1 and 1 hdc) in each of next 2 dc, (ch 1 and 1 sc) in each of next 2 dc, ch 1, a sl st in 2nd st of turning ch; break off.

RIGHT FRONT: Work same as Left Front.

BLOCKING: SEE PAGE 41   CHART : SEE PAGE 106

JOINING OF SECTIONS

Using a darning needle and same material, overcast back and fronts together across shoulders and at underarms.

BORDER

1ST ROUND: Working along opposite side of foundation chain, join yarn with a sl st in first ch st on back section, ch 5, skip next space, 1 dc in same st as next dc of 1st row of back, work (ch 2, skip next space, 1 dc in same st as next dc of 1st row) across back and right front to within next corner space, ch 2, skip 2 sts, work (1 dc, ch 4 and 1 dc) all in corner st; working along ends of rows and placing sts in either top of end dc, or in 3rd st of turning chain, work (ch 2 and 1 dc) in end st of each row along front edge to shoulder seam; working along back of neck ch 2, 1 dc over end st of shoulder row, (ch 2 and 1 dc) in each free dc across back, ch 2, 1 dc over end st of next shoulder row, ch 1, 1 dc in top of last row of other front; work along left front edges to correspond with opposite front, ending with ch 2, a sl st in 3rd st of ch-5 at beginning of this round.

2ND ROUND: Ch 1, *2 sc in each space to next corner space, 4 sc in corner space; repeat from * once, 2 sc in each of remaining spaces, a sl st in first sc of round. A number of sc divisible by 3 is required for next round, if necessary to obtain this, work 3 sc (instead of 2 sc in one or two spaces.

3RD ROUND: Ch 3, work a 2-joined dc over next 2 sc as follows: work (yarn over hook, draw up a loop in next sc, yarn over and draw thru 2 loops) twice, yarn over and draw thru all 3 loops on hook; *ch 5, work a 3-joined dc over next 3 sc as follows: work (yarn over hook, draw up a loop in next sc, yarn over hook and draw thru 2 loops) 3 times, yarn over and draw thru all 4 loops on hook; repeat from * around, ending with ch 5, a sl st in top of first 2-joined dc st.

4TH ROUND: Ch 3, 1 dc in same st as last sl st, *(1 sc in center st of next chain loop, 2 dc in next 3-joined dc) across to next corner, 1 sc in center st of next chain loop, 4 dc in corner st; repeat from * once, then continue to work (1 sc in center st of ch loop, 2 dc in next joined st) around, ending with a sl st in top st of ch-3.

5TH ROUND: Ch 1, 1 sc in same st as last sl st, 1 sc in each st around, a sl st in first sc of round; break off.

ARMHOLE EDGING: Join yarn with 1 sc in first space on last row made before Armholes on back, work 1 more sc in same space, 2 sc in each of next 2 spaces; working along ends of rows, work 2 sc over end of each row along entire armhole edge, ending with 2 sc in each of 3 remaining spaces on last row made before armhole on front, a sl st in first sc; break off.

Work along other armhole edge to correspond.

PATTERN STITCH

VEST
(FOR DAUGHTER'S SIZES)

BACK—1ST ROW: Ch 53 for Size 2-4 (ch 65 for Size 6-8; ch 77 for Size 10-12); this chain should measure, without stretching, 12 inches for Size 2-4 (14-1/2 inches for Size 6-8; 17 inches for Size 10-12); work same as 1st row of Back for Mother's Vest. There are 16 spaces for Size 2-4 (20 for Size 6-8; 24 for Size 10-12).

Repeat 2nd row of Back for Mother's Vest 12 times in all for Size 2-4 (14 times for Size 6-8; 19 times for Size 10-12).

ARMHOLES—1ST ROW: Turn, a sl st in each of first 4 sts, ch 4, 1 dc in next dc, *ch 2, 1 dc in next dc; repeat from *across to within last 2 spaces, ch 1, 1 dc in next dc; do not work over remaining space.

2ND THROUGH 5TH ROWS: Follow directions for 2nd through 5th rows of Back Armholes for Mother's Vest. There are 12 spaces in last row for Size 2-4 (16 for Size 6-8; 20 for Size 10-12).

FOR SIZES 6-8 AND 10-12 ONLY—6TH, 7TH AND 8TH ROWS: Repeat 3rd, 4th and 5th rows of Back Armholes once (there are 14 spaces for Size 6-8; 18 for Size 10-12).

FOR ALL SIZES: Repeat 3rd row of Armholes 3 times for Size 2-4 (once for Size 6-8; 3 times for Size 10-12).

SHOULDERS—NEXT ROW: Turn, a sl st in first dc, work (ch 1 and 1 sc) in each of next 2 dc, work (ch 1 and 1 dc) in each of next 2 dc for Size 2-4 (in each of 3 dc for Sizes 6-8 and 10-12); break off. Skip next 4 spaces for Sizes 2-4 and 6-8 (skip 6 spaces for Size 10-12), join yarn with a sl st in next dc, ch 4, 1 dc in next dc, (For Sizes 6-8 and 10-12 Only—ch 1, 1 dc in next dc), For All Sizes—work (ch 1 and 1 sc) in each of next 2 dc, ch 1, a sl st in 2nd st of turning ch; break off.

LEFT FRONT—1ST ROW: Ch 29 for Size 2-4 (ch 32 for Size 6-8; ch 35 for Size 10-12); this chain should measure, without stretching, 6 inches for Size 2-4 (7 inches for Size 6-8; 8 inches for Size 10-12); work same as first row of Back for Mother's Vest. There are 8 spaces in row for Size 2-4 (9 for Size 6-8; 10 for Size 10-12).
Repeat 2nd row of Back for Mother's Vest 12 times in all for Size 2-4 (14 times for Size 6-8; 19 times for Size 10-12).

ARMHOLE—1ST ROW: Turn, a sl st in each of first 4 sts, ch 4, 1 dc in next dc, *ch 2, 1 dc in next dc; repeat from * across row, ending with ch 2, 1 dc in 3rd st of turning chain. There are 7 spaces in row for Size 2-4 (8 for Size 6-8; 9 for Size 10-12).
2ND THROUGH 6TH ROWS: Repeat 2nd through 6th rows of Left Front Armhole for Mother's Vest.

FOR SIZE 2-4 ONLY—7TH AND 8TH ROWS: Repeat 3rd and 4th rows of Left Front Armhole of Mother's Vest.

FOR SIZE 6-8 ONLY—7TH THROUGH 10TH ROWS: Repeat 3rd through 6th rows of Left Front Armhole of Mother's Vest.

FOR SIZE 10-12 ONLY—7TH THROUGH 12TH ROWS: Repeat 3rd through 6th rows of Left Front Armhole of Mother's Vest once, then repeat 3rd and 4th rows of same Armhole once more.

FOR ALL SIZES—SHOULDER: Turn, a sl st in first dc, work (ch 1, skip next space, 1 sc in next dc) twice, (ch 1 and 1 dc) in each of remaining dc, 1 dc in 2nd st of turning chain; break off.

RIGHT FRONT: Work same as Left Front, Starting from Blocking, complete Vest same as for Mother's Vest.

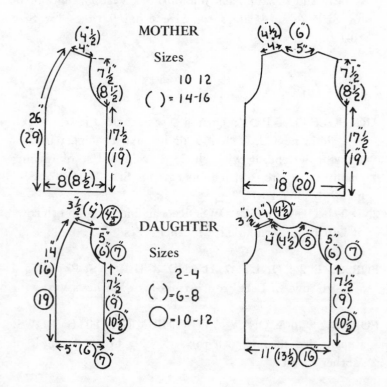

MOTHER

Sizes

10 12

( ) = 14-16

DAUGHTER

Sizes

2-4

( ) = 6-8

◯ = 10-12

FATHER AND SON VESTS

MATERIALS NEEDED AND SIZES

Original garments were made of Marvel-Twist (4-ply Knitting Worsted).				
Vest	Size	Material	Quantity	Crochet Hook
For Father	36-38	4-ply Knitting Worsted	16 ounces	No. 9 or I Plastic
	40-42		20 ounces	
For Son	4-6		8 ounces	
	8-10		10 ounces	
	12-14		12 ounces	

Four 3/4″ buttons are required for Father's Vest.
Four 5/8″ buttons are required for Son's Vest.

Gauge – Working in Pattern Stitch
3 crossed dc groups (6 dc) = 2 inches.
4 rows = 2-1/2 inches.

VEST
(FOR FATHER'S SIZE)

BACK–1ST ROW: Ch 59 for Size 36-38 (ch 63 for Size 40-42); this chain should measure without stretching, 20 inches for Size 36-38 (21 inches for Size 40-42), 1 dc in 5th st from hook, work a crossed over dc in 4th st from hook as follows: yarn over hook, insert hook from front to back in 4th st from hook, yarn over hook and working over dc, just completed, draw up a loop and complete dc (see Detail 1); this completes a 2 crossed dc group; *skip 1 ch st, 1 dc in next ch st, a crossed dc (same as before) in skipped chain st (this completes another 2 crossed dc group);repeat from * across row, ending with a 2 crossed dc group over last 2 chain sts. There are 28 (2 crossed dc groups) in row for Size 36-38 (30 for Size 40-42).

2ND ROW: Ch 3, turn, skip first 2 dc, 1 dc in next dc, a crossed over dc in skipped dc (next to dc just completed) *a 2 crossed dc group over next 2 dc (see Detail 2);repeat from * across row, ending with a 2 crossed dc group in top st of turning chain and last dc of row below. Last row forms Pattern stitch.

Repeat last row 27 more times for all sizes.

1

2

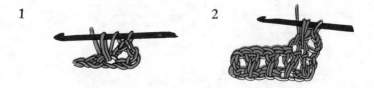

ARMHOLE—1ST ROW: Turn, a sl st in each of first 4 sts, ch 3, skip 1 dc, *a 2 crossed dc group over next 2 sts; repeat from *23 times for Size 36-38 (25 times for Size 40-42); do not work over remaining sts.

2ND ROW: Turn, skip first 2 sts, a sl st in next st, ch 3, *a 2 crossed dc group over next 2 sts; repeat from * 21 times for Size 36-38 (23 times for Size 40-42); end with 1 dc in last dc.

3RD ROW: Ch 3, turn, skip first 2 dc, *a 2 crossed dc group over next 2 sts; repeat from * across row, end same as in 2nd Row of Pattern Stitch.

Repeat 2nd Row of Pattern Stitch 12 times for Size 36-38 (14 times for Size 40-42).

SHOULDERS—1ST ROW: Turn, a sl st in each of first 5 sts; *a 2 crossed dc group over next 2 sts; repeat from * 16 times for Size 36-38 (18 times for Size 40-42), end with skip a st, 1 sc in next st; do not work over remaining sts.

2ND ROW: Ch 1, turn, skip first st, a sl st in each of next 3 sts; *a 2 crossed dc group over next 2 sts; repeat from * across to 5 end sts of last row, 1 sc in next st; do not work over remaining sts.

Repeat last row; break off.

LEFT FRONT—1ST ROW: Ch 41 for Size 36-38 (ch 45 for Size 40-42); this chain should measure without stretching 13" for Size 36-38 (14" for Size 40-42), 1 dc in 5th st from hook work a crossed over dc in 4th st from hook; *work a 2 crossed dc group over next 2 sts; repeat from * across row. There are 19 (2 crossed dc groups) in row for Size 36-38 (21 for Size 40-42).

Repeat 2nd row of Back (Pattern Stitch) 25 more times for all sizes.

1ST DECREASING ROW: Ch 3, turn, skip first st; *a 2 crossed dc group over next 2 sts; repeat from * across to last dc, end with 1 dc in last dc; do not work in top of turning chain (this decreases one st at Front Edge).

2ND DECREASING ROW: Ch 3, turn, skip first 2 sts; *a 2 crossed dc group over next 2 sts; repeat from * across row, end same as in 2nd row of Pattern Stitch.

3RD DECREASING ROW: Repeat 1st Decreasing Row.

ARMHOLE AND NECK, EDGE—1ST ROW: Ch 3, turn, skip first 2 sts; *a 2 crossed dc group over next 2 sts; repeat from * across to last 4 sts (counting turning ch 3 as last st); do not work over remaining sts.

2ND ROW: Turn, skip first 2 sts, a sl st in next st, ch 3, *a 2 crossed dc group over next 2 sts; repeat from * across to last dc, end with 1 dc in last dc.

3RD ROW: Ch 3, turn, skip first 2 sts, *a 2 crossed dc group over next 2 sts; repeat from * across to last dc, end with 1 dc in last dc.

4TH ROW: Repeat last row.

Repeat 2nd and 1st Decreasing Rows 4 times for Size 36-38 (6 times for Size 40-42).

Repeat 2nd Decreasing Row once more.

Repeat 2nd row of Pattern Stitch twice for <u>Size 36-38 Only</u>.

SHOULDER—1ST ROW: Turn, a sl st in each of first 5 sts, (a 2 crossed dc group over next 2 sts) 5 times.

2ND ROW: Ch 3, turn, skip first st (a 2 crossed dc group over next 2 sts) twice, 1 sc in next st; break off.

RIGHT FRONT: Repeat 1st row of Left Front.
Repeat 2nd row of Pattern stitch 24 times.
Repeat 1st and 2nd decreasing rows twice.

ARMHOLE AND NECK EDGE—1ST ROW: Turn, a sl st in
each of first 4 sts, ch 3, skip 1 dc, *a 2 crossed dc group
over next 2 sts; repeat from * across to last dc, end with 1
dc in last dc.
2ND ROW: Ch 3, turn, skip first 2 sts, *a 2 crossed dc group
over next 2 sts; repeat from * across to last dc, end with 1
dc in last dc.
3RD ROW: Ch 3, turn, skip first 2 dc a 2 crossed dc group
over next 2 sts; repeat from * across to last dc, end with 1
dc in last dc.
4TH ROW: Ch 3, turn, skip first 2 sts, *a 2 crossed dc group
over next 2 sts; repeat from * across row.
Repeat 1st and 2nd Decreasing Rows 5 times for Size
36-38 (6 times for Size 40-42).
Repeat 2nd row of Pattern Stitch once more.

SHOULDER—1ST ROW: Ch 3, turn, skip first st, *a 2
crossed dc group over next 2 sts; repeat from *3 times,
skip 1 st, 1 sc in next st.
2ND ROW: Ch 1, turn, skip first st, a sl st in each of next 3
sts, *a 2 crossed dc group over next 2 sts, repeat from *
twice; break off.

BLOCKING: SEE PAGE 41.

JOINING OF SECTIONS: Using a darning needle and same
yarn overcast back and front sections together across
shoulders and at underarms.

BUTTON AND BUTTONHOLE BORDER (Father and Son's Vests)—

1ST ROW: Starting at front corner of Left Front and holding wrong side of work toward you, join yarn with an sc in first foundation chain, work 2 sc over each end dc of rows and each turning (ch 3) along left front to back neck edge, work 1 sc in each dc to right front edge, 2 sc over each end dc of rows and each turning (ch 3) to bottom of right front, ending with 1 sc in foundation chain.

2ND ROW: Ch 1, turn, 1 sc in each sc of last row.

3RD ROW: (BUTTONHOLES)—Ch 1, turn, 1 sc in each of first 2 sc, *ch 2, skip next 2 sc for buttonhole, 1 sc in each of next 14 sc for Father's Vest, (8 sc for Size 4-6; 9 sc for Size 8-10; 10 sc for Size 12-14) for Son's Vest; repeat from * twice, ch 2, skip next 2 sc, 1 sc in each remaining sc of row.

1ST ROUND: Ch 1, turn, 2 sc in first sc, *1 sc in each sc up to (ch 2) for buttonhole, 2 sc in (ch 2) space; repeat from * 3 times, 1 sc in next sc, 3 sc in next corner sc, 1 sc in end sc's of next 2 rows, working along opposite side of foundation chain (bottom edge), 1 sc in each ch st up sc rows, 1 sc in each end sc of next 2 rows, 1 more sc in same st as first 2 sc of round, a sl st in top of first sc of round.

2ND ROUND: Ch 1 (do not turn) 3 sc in same sc as sl st (corner sc) 1 sc in each sc up to next corner sc, 3 sc in corner sc, 1 sc in each remaining sc of round, a sl st in top of first sc of round; break off.

ARMHOLE BORDER—1ST ROUND: Holding right side of work toward you, join yarn with an sc in dc next to underarm seam, work 1 sc in each dc, 2 sc over each (ch 3) and 2 sc over each end dc of rows all around armhole edge, end with a sl st in top of first sc of round.

2ND ROUND: Ch 1, 1 sc in each sc of round, **end** same as before; break off.

Finish other armhole in same manner.

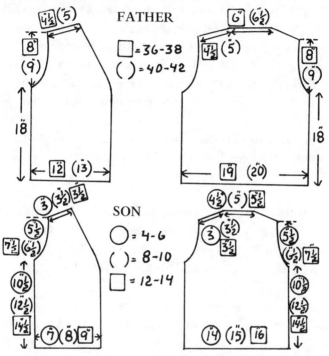

Detail of Pattern Stitch

VEST
(FOR SON'S SIZE)

BACK—1ST ROW: Ch 47 for Size 4-6 (ch 51 for Size 8-10; ch 55 for Size 12-14); this chain should measure without stretching 15 inches for Size 4-6 (16 inches for Size 8-10; 17 inches for Size 12-14); work same as first row of Back for Father's Vest. There are 22 (2 crossed dc groups) for Size 4-6, (24 groups for Size 8-10; 26 groups for Size 12-14).

Repeat 2nd row of Back for Father's Vest 17 times for Size 4-6 (21 times for Size 8-10; 25 times for Size 12-14, or desired length to armhole).

ARMHOLES—1ST ROW: Turn, a sl st in each of first 4 sts, ch 3, skip 1 dc *a 2 crossed dc group over next 2 sts; repeat from * 17 times for Size 4-6 (19 times for Size 8-10; 21 times for Size 12-14); do not work over remaining sts.

2ND ROW: Turn, skip first 2 sts, a sl st in next st, ch 3, *a 2 crossed dc group over next 2 sts; repeat from * 15 times for Size 4-6 (17 times for Size 8-10; 19 times for Size 12-14).

Repeat 2nd row of Back of Father's Vest 7 times for Size 4-6 (9 times for Size 8-10; 11 times for Size 12-14).

SHOULDERS—FOR ALL SIZES—1ST ROW: Turn, a sl st in each of first 5 sts, *a 2 crossed dc group over next 2 sts; repeat from * across to 6 end sts of last row, counting ch 3 as a st, 1 sc in next st; do not work over remaining sts.

2ND ROW: Ch 1, turn, skip first st, a sl st in each of next 3 sts; *a 2 crossed dc group over next 2 sts; repeat from * across to 5 end sts, 1 sc in next st; break off for all sizes.

LEFT FRONT—1ST ROW: Ch 25 for Size 4-6 (ch 29 for Size 8-10; ch 33 for Size 12-14) this chain should measure without stretching 8" for Size 4-6 (9" for Size 8-10; 10" for Size 12-14); work same as first row of Left Front of Father's Vest; there are 11 (2 crossed dc groups) in row for Size 4-6 (13 for Size 8-10; 15 for Size 12-14).

Repeat 2nd row of Left Front of Father's Vest 15 times for Size 4-6 (19 times for Size 8-10; 23 times for Size 12-14) or desired length to armhole to correspond with Back.

Repeat 1st, 2nd and 3rd decreasing rows of Left Front of Father's Vest, also 1st and 2nd rows of armhole and neck edge.

Repeat 2nd and 1st Decreasing Rows.

Repeat 2nd Decreasing Row once more for all sizes.

Repeat 1st and 2nd Decreasing Rows twice more for Size 12-14.

Repeat 2nd row of Pattern Stitch 4 times for Sizes 4-6; 12-14; (6 times for Size 8-10).

SHOULDERS (ALL SIZES):

1ST ROW: Turn, a sl st in each of first 5 sts; *a 2 crossed dc group over next 2 sts; repeat from * across row; break off for Size 4-6 only.

2ND ROW—FOR SIZE 8-10; 12-14 ONLY: Ch 3, turn, skip first st, a 2 crossed dc group over next 2 sts, 1 sc in next st; break off.

RIGHT FRONT—Repeat 1st row of Left Front.

Repeat 2nd row of Left Front 14 times for Size 4-6 (18 times for Size 8-10; 22 times for Size 12-14) or desired length to correspond with Left Front.

Repeat 1st and 2nd Decreasing Rows of Left Front of Father's Vest twice, also repeat 1st, 2nd, 3rd and 4th rows of Armhole and Neck Edge of Right Front of Father's Vest for Sizes 4-6; 8-10.

FOR SIZE 12-14 ONLY: Repeat 1st and 2nd Decreasing rows twice more.
Repeat 2nd row of Pattern Stitch 5 times for Size 4-6; 12-14 and 7 times for Size 8-10.

SHOULDERS—SIZE 4-6—1ST ROW: Ch 3, turn, skip first st, a 2 crossed dc group over next 2 sts, 1 sc in next st; break off.
FOR SIZES 8-10; 12-14—1ST ROW: Ch 3, turn, skip first st, *a 2 crossed dc group over next 2 sts; repeat from * to last 6 sts (counting ch 3 as 1 st) 1 sc in next st; break off.
FOR ALL SIZES—2ND ROW: Turn, skip first st, a sl st in each of next 3 sts, 1 sc in next st, 1 dc in next st, a 2 crossed dc group over next 2 sts.

BLOCKING: Same as Father's Vest.

JOINING OF SECTIONS: Same as Father's Vest.

BUTTON AND BUTTONHOLE BORDER: See Father's Vest.

ARMHOLE BORDER: See Father's Vest.

FLOWER AFGHAN

MATERIALS NEEDED AND SIZES

4 ply Knitting Worsted.

Each Medallion (5 inches diagonally from point to point) takes about 11-1/2 yards of one color; 7 yards of contrasting color.

Article	Afghan	Pillow	Crochet Hook
Size	45 × 62 Inches	13 Inches in Diameter	No. 6 or G Plastic
Material Needed	35 ozs. of scraps or 9 ozs. each of 4 colors and 20 ozs. of contrasting color for edging	2 ozs. of scraps and 1 oz. of contrasting color for edging	No. 6 or G Plastic
No. of Medallions	149	7	

COLOR CHART

For afghan in a combination of four
(or less) colors; plus edging.
Either all four colors or first two or three
colors suggested can be used; as desired.

First Color	Second Color	Third Color	Fourth Color	Edging
Beige	Red	Light Grey	Dark Grey	Black
Light Rose	Medium Rose	Dark Rose	Lavender	Purple
Yellow	Light Blue	Gold	Dark Blue	Brown
Light Blue	Pink	Delft Blue	Dark Rose	Dark Grey

AFGHAN
FIRST MEDALLION

1ST ROUND: With first color, ch 5, join with a sl st into a ring, ch 3, 1 dc into ring, *ch 3, 2 dc into ring; repeat from * 4 more times, ch 3, a sl st in top st of ch 3 at the beginning of round, (there are 6 groups in round).

2ND ROUND: A sl st in next dc, a sl st in next (ch 3) loop, ch 3, 4 dc in same (ch 3) loop as last sl st, *skip next 2 dc, 5 dc in next (ch 3) loop; repeat from * around, end with a sl st in top st of ch 3 at beginning of round.

3RD ROUND: A sl st in next dc, ch 3, 5 dc in next dc, 1 dc in next dc, *skip next 2 dc, 1 dc in next dc, 5 dc in next dc, 1 dc in next dc; repeat from * around, end with a sl st in top st of ch 3 at the beginning of round, (there are 6 petals in round); break off.

EDGING

With contrasting color (same color should be used for edging on all medallions), join yarn with 1 sc in same st as end sl st of last round, 1 sc in next dc, 2 sc in each of next 3 dc, 1 sc in each of next 2 dc, ch 6, working in front of last round work 1 sc around front loops at base of (2 dc) group below on first round as follows: insert hook under second loop at base of first dc of (2 dc) group below, also insert hook under first loop at base of next dc on same group, yarn over hook, draw up a loop under loops on hook, yarn over and thru 2 loops on hook, *ch 6, 1 sc in each of next 2 dc on last round, 2 sc in each of next 3 dc, 1 sc in each of next 2 dc, ch 6, working in front of last round work 1 sc around front loops at base of next (2 dc) group below on first round; repeat from * around, end last repeat with ch 6, 1 sc around front loops of starting ch and first dc on first round, ch 6, a sl st in first sc at the beginning of round.

If scraps of many colors are being used, having a different color (in place of first color) for each medallion, but always having same (dark) color for edging on all medallions, make 142 more medallions following directions for First Medallion (143 medallions in all).

If four or less colors are being used for entire afghan, crochet as close to the same number of medallions as possible of each color, making 143 medallions in all.

BLOCKING: SEE PAGE 41

Stretch and pin each medallion to the correct size and shape on a padded surface; cover with a damp cloth; steam (do not press) with a warm iron. Remove when dry.

JOINING OF MEDALLIONS

Pick up two medallions of different colors; using a darning needle and same color as edgings of medallions, skip first 5 sc on edging of first medallion, overcast following 4 sc (from A to B on Illustration of Medallion); fasten off. Skip first sc on next petal of first medallion, overcast following 4 sc (from C to D on Illustration) to corresponding sts on next medallion. Arranging colors as desired, place third medallion next to second medallion, opposite joined petals. Skip petal before joining on second medallion, skip first 5 sc on next petal, overcast following 4 sc to corresponding sc on third medallion; skip first sc on next petal of second medallion; overcast following 4 sc to corresponding sc on third medallion.

Continue to join medallions in a row until 10 medallions have been joined.

Medallions are joined in rows; then rows are joined together.

Make 7 more rows of 10 medallions in each row. Make 7 rows of 9 medallions in each row. Arrange rows as shown on Chart for Joining and join rows together.

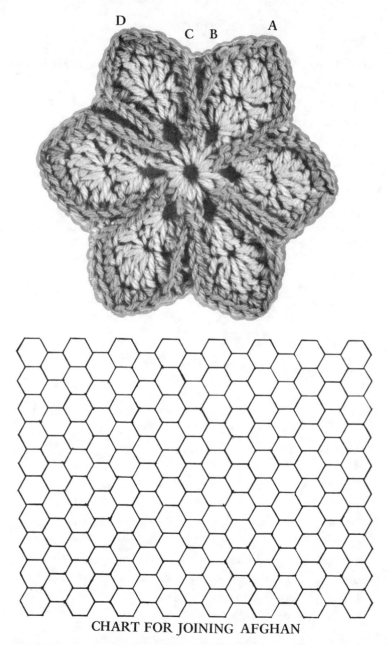

D   C   B   A

CHART FOR JOINING AFGHAN

PILLOW

Make 7 medallions, following directions for First Medallion
for Afghan.
Joining as for Afghan, join medallions in a row of three and
two rows of two in each row (see Chart for Pillow).

BLOCKING CHART

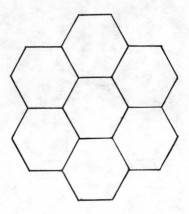

TO MAKE PILLOW

A round foundation pillow 13 inches in diameter and two
pieces of lining material 1/2 inch larger all around are
needed. Seam lining pieces together, leaving a large
opening and making 1/4 inch seam; turn right side out, slip
foundation pillow in casing, overcast across opening. Tack
crochet to top of pillow.

CROCHETED BAG

MATERIALS NEEDED AND SIZES

Original Bag made of Spinnerin Mardi Gras Yarn (100% Polypropylene).

Article	Material	Quantity	Crochet Hook
Handbag	Straw Yarn in 110 yd. balls	3 balls	No. 6 or G Plastic

Also, a metal weight chain about 24" long to be used for handle; 3/8 yard buckram for interlining; 3/4 yard of 35" lining material, matching sewing thread, and 2 large, covered snap fasteners.

GAUGE
7 sc = 2 inches;   10 rows = 3 inches

1ST ROW: Ch 44 (this chain should measure 12-1/2 inches without stretching), 1 sc in 2nd st from hook, 1 sc in each of remaining 42 sts of chain.

2ND ROW: Ch 1, turn, 1 sc in each of 43 sc of last row.

Repeat 2nd row 66 times.

69TH ROW (FLAP): Ch 1, turn, work a 2 joined sc over first 2 sts as follows: Insert hook in first st of last row, yarn over hook, pull loop through st on hook, insert hook in next st, yarn over hook, draw up a loop in next st, yarn over hook and thru all 3 loops on hook, 1 sc in each sc to last 2 sts, a 2 joined sc over last 2 sts.

Repeat 69th row 10 times, break off.

EDGING FOR SHAPED FLAP: Join yarn with an sc over 2 joined sc at end of 69th row, 1 sc over end st of each of next 10 rows, 1 sc in each sc of last row, 1 sc over end st of each of next 11 rows; break off.

GUSSET—1ST ROW: Ch 6, 1 sc in 2nd st from hook, 1 sc in each of next 4 sts of chain.

2ND ROW: Ch 1, turn, 1 sc in each sc of last row.

Repeat 2nd row 3 times.

6TH ROW: Ch 1, turn, 2 sc in first sc, 1 sc in each of remaining 4 sc.

7TH ROW: Same as 2nd row.

8TH ROW: Same as 2nd row.

9TH ROW: Ch 1, turn, 2 sc in first sc, 1 sc in each of remaining 5 sc.

10TH ROW: Same as 2nd row.

11TH ROW: Same as 2nd row.

12TH ROW: Ch 1, turn, 2 sc in first sc, 1 sc in each of remaining 6 sc.

13TH, 14TH, 15TH AND 16TH ROWS: Same as 2nd row.

17TH ROW: Ch 1, turn, a 2 joined sc over first 2 sts, 1 sc in each of remaining sc.

18TH ROW: Ch 1, turn, 1 sc in each sc across row, 1 sc in 2 joined sc.

Repeat 17th and 18th rows twice; break off.

Face each gusset with lining material, cuttting lining material 1/2" longer than crocheted piece.

DETAIL OF PATTERN STITCH

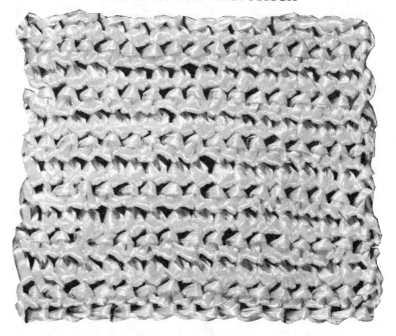

JOINING OF SECTIONS: Pin 1st row of gusset and bag together; pin opposite side of 1st row of gusset to 54th row of bag. Using same straw yarn overcast side edges and last row of gusset to side rows of bag.

LINING: Using crocheted bag as a pattern piece cut two pieces of lining material 1/2 inch larger all around. Cut one piece buckram same size as bag. With wrong side facing sew lining together making 1/2 inch seams along three sides (two long sides and flap). Turn right side out, slip buckram inside lining; turn 1/2 inch to inside at opening and overcast edges together. Slip stitch lining to inside of bag allowing crochet to extend about 1/8 inch all around.

HANDLE: Using same straw yarn and crochet hook as used for bag, make a chain about 3" longer than metal chain, work 1 dc in 4th st from hook, 1 dc in each st across chain. Break off. Weave metal chain thru crochet, having groups of 2 dc over and under crochet. Stitch each end of handle to center of each gusset, placing handle about 1" from top edge. Sew snap fasteners to flap.

EXTRA   EXTRA   EXTRA   EXTRA

4 INSTANT BOOKS

Order additional copies now.

for   A friend

A school

Your church

Gifts

or to replace the copy your friends will "borrow" from you.

SEND $1. FOR EACH COPY of
INSTANT SEWING
INSTANT FASHION
INSTANT CROCHET
INSTANT MACRAMÉ

NAME OF YOUR PUBLICATION
INSTANT BOOKS
Box 155, Old Chelsea Station
New York, N.Y. 10011

In Canada:
NAME OF YOUR PUBLICATION
INSTANT BOOKS
60 Progress Avenue
Scarborough, Ontario
M1T 4P7

Please add 25¢ for postage and handling for each book.